Something

to Hold

Onto

Simple Metaphors, Images, and
Practical Tools to Transform Your Life

KATE ROBSON

Introduction by Sarah Polley
With illustrations by Sebastian Frye

Published by Simon & Schuster

New York Amsterdam/Antwerp London Toronto Sydney/Melbourne New Delhi

SIMON &
SCHUSTER
CANADA

A Division of Simon & Schuster, LLC
166 King Street East, Suite 300
Toronto, Ontario M5A 1J3

This Simon & Schuster Canada edition January 2026

Interior design by Ruth Lee-Mui
Illustrations by Sebastian Frye

Manufactured in the United States of America

1   3   5   7   9   10   8   6   4   2

Online Computer Library Center number: 1523195176

ISBN 978-1-6680-9187-6
ISBN 978-1-6680-9361-0 (ebook)

To my mother, Wendy, who taught me how to show up.

To my father, Stuart, who found something
delightful and interesting in everyone.

I miss and love you both so much.

Contents

Imagine . . .

Introduction

A few years ago, I was in serious crisis. I'll spare you the details, but my body and brain had gone into a violent stress spiral that I couldn't see a way out of. I'm not great at letting people know when I'm doing poorly, so when my good friend Kate Robson called me and asked how I was doing, I casually mentioned that I was okay despite having a bit of a tough time. Until that moment, no one had been able to hear the deep distress and panic behind my assurances that I was okay.

A few minutes after I hung up the phone, I got a text from Kate. "I just have a funny feeling, and I'm a bit worried about you. I'm going to be there in ten minutes. I hope that's okay."

For four days I had been having an almost continuous panic attack. My heart raced, I had a hard time breathing, and I had a sickening numb feeling in my legs. Kate walked into my house, gave me a hug, and asked if there was someplace quiet where we could talk. She asked me if I'd be open to an experiment. I could hardly make a sound and was flooded with tears. But I nodded. Here was Kate, showing up, right on time and right on brand, and I was so very grateful.

Kate led me through some visualization exercises using a few of the images that she has written about so eloquently in this book. I discovered, with her guidance, a beautiful place in my mind that

I could return to in times of stress. I developed a toolbox of strategies that helped me regulate my emotions and bring me "down the ladder" as she describes in one chapter. After fifteen minutes, I was okay. And okay was a long way from where I had been such a short time ago. What I suddenly knew—and had not known before she arrived bearing her incredible gift of images—was that I would survive. It's how I feel every time I read this book, as though someone has handed me a toolbox with a beautifully written instruction manual, complete with diagrams to address (and often fix) all of the problems in my house.

I've known Kate for many years, and if there is one quality that I associate with her more than any other, it is her consistency in really showing up for other people. This book offers a window into the inner work it takes to become someone with this gift of stability and presence. In many ways, it feels like a how-to manual for becoming the kind of person who is capable of supporting themselves and the people around them in difficult times, just as Kate does so expertly in her everyday life.

I'm lucky enough to have Kate drop by when I'm struggling and to get to go for walks with her often as we ramble through the messy middle of our unfolding lives. It's such a gift to experience her curiosity and deep investment in the people who cross her path. Often, when I meet someone who is struggling, I wish so badly for them to have a Kate Robson in their lives. With this book, I am thrilled that so many people now have access to her compassion, wisdom, and humour as well as to the tools she has honed for many years as a therapist, parent support worker in an NICU, mother, and friend.

Unlike so many self-help books I've read in the past, the visual nature of the tools Kate offers here have staying power. I often find myself transformed by a book, only to forget its contents when I need it the most. With *Something to Hold Onto*, Kate gives us exactly that. When the world is spinning chaotically around you, and you can't remember the words to reach for, I find it's surprisingly easy to return to these transformative images and suddenly find myself back within these comforting pages.

For example, I often find myself checking to make sure the "adult is driving the bus" or that I'm scattering small joys to look forward to like a "string of lights" during tough times. I've learned from this book to ask myself where I need to be right now and "what is this in service of?"

These images and questions have become a part of my everyday programming, both at work and at home.

At its heart, I think of this book as an invitation to play, to experiment and get to know yourself and discover what works. It is an offering of images that can make all the difference when we need it the most.

Now, when I meet someone who is having a hard time, I am relieved to be able to hand them this book, which is akin to handing them forty walks with Kate. This is, in my opinion, all we really need to survive.

—SARAH POLLEY

A note before we begin

For the entirety of my time as a therapist in private practice, and even before that, when I was supporting families in the neonatal intensive care unit (NICU), I have found that images and metaphors can help us free ourselves from a constricting thought or judgment, and can help us get to know and respect our own experience a bit more. Let me show you what I mean.

Imagine a person coming into a therapist's office full of feelings they can't even name. They share some details about why they're having a hard time and then immediately burst into an explanation of why they aren't, in fact, entitled to be having a hard time. Other people have it harder! They are very lucky! Why, then, are they feeling so bad? They feel so much guilt for experiencing pain and even more guilt for needing to talk about it with someone. The guilt then becomes the pain they want to talk about, and it crowds everything else out of the room.

In an effort to loosen the grip of that guilt, the therapist could use words and logic to try to convince them that their suffering is important and that their feelings matter. They might also say something like the following.

"Do you ever go to the grocery store intending to pick up just one thing? And when you get there you remember you need all sorts of other things and end up with two huge heavy bags. If you have to walk any kind of distance with these bags, they start getting heavy. It might feel like your arms are stretching." At this point the person might chime in with their own story of when they helped a friend move or packed too much into a suitcase.

"When we notice this, we might push through for a while (and regret it the next day), but often we'll give ourselves a rest. We'll put the bags down and take a breath or two. If we're really having a hard time, we might ask for help. But we probably wouldn't spend a lot of time telling ourselves that what we're feeling isn't real or that we don't get to feel it."

This might be when the person nods their head.

"So maybe that's what you're doing today. You're noticing that you've been carrying something really heavy, and you're taking an opportunity to put it down for a moment, to rest, to ask for help, and to look at exactly what you're carrying. And then maybe you get to choose what you pick back up again."

And maybe—not always, but often—this everyday ordinary image helps them start talking about what is so heavy, how it feels, and what they're willing to carry, and they can leave the guilt and justification behind at the side of the road.

It took me a long time to feel like I could come into a therapist's office and put down, even for a moment, what I was finding heavy and what I was holding onto so tightly. For most of my life, until well into my forties, I attributed sadness, anxiety, or low mood to personal weakness or a temporary (if regrettable) response to crisis. When my sister and I were teenagers, our mother's response to any complicated feelings was to listen to us for ten minutes, and then lovingly tell us, "Buck up and move on!" She died when I was nineteen, and while I couldn't quite buck up and move on, I did go right back to school, carrying my grief and rage with me. I loved her so much. I still love her so much.

And I kept on moving. I graduated, travelled, quit jobs and took jobs, and moved a world away to another country and another culture, perhaps trying to run away from my own sadness and fear. When that fairy tale turned farce ended, I came back home, met someone wonderful, and got married. I felt for a moment like I'd moved past suffering and into contentment. Then came miscarriage and a complicated pregnancy and then the very early birth of an impossibly tiny baby. We all survived that, and in due course I had another slightly less impossibly tiny baby (but still so very tiny) and ended up hospitalized myself with kidney failure. I didn't have time to be sick, though, with a baby in intensive care and a toddler at home, so I made use of my old friends, repression and denial. I bucked up and moved on. My ability to do so became a rigid part of my identity that I latched onto with an iron grip.

Once we were all out of hospital and settling in at home, I found myself at times consumed with anxiety; I felt such shame about it that I couldn't really articulate it to anyone around me. We were the lucky ones! Our babies had survived, and I had survived, and we were all okay. What was wrong with me that at times I couldn't breathe or that I was preoccupied and sometimes immobilized with fear about improbable dangers visiting my little family? Why couldn't I move past these terrible things I was feeling?

In search of meaning, I went back to work in the NICU that had cared for my first baby. It's an incredible, impossible place, full of the smallest people and the biggest stories. I loved (and still love) the team of people who work there. These are people who've figured out how to enter a gladiator's arena every day and fight for other people's lives. I'm so grateful to them for it, so blown away—and I also worry for them because, of course, all of that comes at a cost that they are left to carry without much in the way of support or recognition. In any case, it was an honour to spend time there. I felt the work was so meaningful, and I hoped that it would help transform my relationship with anxiety and sadness. Then came a day when I started experiencing severe chest pains. The pains themselves turned out to be nothing serious, but what stopped me in my tracks was a thought that kept showing up: *Maybe if this is a mild heart attack I could take some time off work.*

Just so you know, if you ever find yourself hoping that you're having a mild heart attack so you can take time off, please take some time off. (And maybe talk to a therapist?)

In the movie version of my life, after a moment like this, things would have moved quickly and decisively, perhaps with a fun make-over scene in the midst. In the real-life messy version, there were some twists, some wrong turns, and some next-level avoidance strategies. I eventually realized that I'd been holding onto an idea of myself so tightly that I was choking the life out of my life. I was so focused on being the person I thought I had to be that I wasn't noticing how I was actually showing up.

An apologetic, ashamed, exhausted me finally took herself to therapy and then to therapy school. In therapy school, I finally stopped moving. I mean, in one sense I was moving all over the place! I was learning, I was connecting, I was understanding, I was changing. But in a way that was utterly transformative for me, I was able to pause. To take a breath. To recognize the weight of what I was carrying. To recognize how I was contributing to that weight, and to put some of it down for a while. I was able start exercising some discernment and some loving thoughtfulness about what I was going to pick up again. I began to bring in a sense of play and wonder even into hard moments, so that I could experiment and practice and hold any outcomes very lightly and with gentle care.

I am so deeply grateful that I was able to come to this place in my life, and I can feel these changes in me rippling out into my relationships, my work, and my world. To feel comfortable in my own skin, to feel familiar with myself, to feel a flexible sense of identity, to have more than a nodding acquaintanceship with my own emotions and values, to be able to exercise some choice and experience some agency, to be able to notice when my own judgments and thoughts are weighing me down, and to be able to breathe lightness and choice into that heaviness all feels like a wonderful gift, and it's a gift I would like to share with you.

How do images and metaphors connect with this idea? How can they help us find this comfort with ourselves, this flexible identity? How might they help us cope with our heaviest burdens? When we find ourselves in a hard moment, in the midst of discomfort or a sadness that we don't understand, we can feel trapped, and so of course we seek escape. We harness our rational brains in search of clarity, certainty, rules, diagnoses, or frameworks, and we hope that these tactics will be enough to erase the fog, banish our pain, and exile our worry. Sometimes they are enough, or at least they do a good enough job of medicating our pain for a while.

Sometimes, maybe even most of the time, the relief is temporary, and we find ourselves trapped again, somewhere with the old pain and the new rules.

Let's try something different. Let's invite other parts of ourselves out to play. Let's use images to engage our imaginations, hit pause on the workings and scheming of our rational brains and the word prisons they can build for us, and embrace uncertainty—a place of maybe.

Uncertainty can be terrifying. Our systems crave certainty, and we will often seek it out even if it comes at a cost of narrowing our lives and experiences. If we think about uncertainty as a place of maybe, it can also be seen as a space, a staging ground, or an opportunity for experimentation and wonder. Images can help us stay in that place; they're easy to remember when we feel lost in storms of emotions or events, and they can serve as something to hold onto, to remind us of who we are and what's important to us.

If you're up for trying something different, let's begin from a very specific, grounded stance. Together, we're going to operate from a place of deep respect and love for ourselves, our histories, our adaptations, and our own wisdom. If we find ourselves feeling uncomfortable directing this kind of love and respect at ourselves, we'll try to hold that discomfort lightly and to be curious about where it might come from. We probably know already, if we slow down and listen.

We don't want to set up new rules for ourselves or replace one false set of certainties for another, so before we start, let's issue ourselves some invitations—to be curious, to be kind, to be attentive, to be intentional.

And now let's see what happens when we let ourselves imagine. Let's say I'm giving you a trunk. It's wooden and has big iron handles and a clunky lock. What might be inside?

Imagine an old trunk

Of course, just because I want to give you a gift doesn't mean you have to take it. I'm sure this has happened to you at some point in your life. Some person, perhaps a beloved person, has given you something. Let's imagine an old trunk that could be filled with treasure or full of garbage. We don't know yet!

Let's imagine looking into the trunk and seeing all sorts of objects piled up on top of each other. Some of them might be genuinely precious to you, things you gleefully pull out and bring close to your heart. These you can accept joyfully.

Other items may not bring you this feeling. Some might have been lovely in the other person's home but have no room in yours. Others might have uncomfortable or even terrible associations for you, like a painting that always scared you as a little kid or a souvenir from a horrible vacation. Those things can get left in the trunk. You don't have to take everything. You actually don't have to take anything if you don't want to.

This is the point that gets uncomfortable for many people. *I'll disappoint the person who wants to give me these things! I'll let them down!* they think. That might be true. The person who's trying to give away these things might have an emotional response to what you do. You can be caring and curious about that, but your main job in that moment is to make honest decisions rooted in your own values.

What are these objects in the trunk? In this context I see them as organizing principles, or our unconscious beliefs and ideas about the world and how it works. Sometimes these are called "iceberg beliefs," because there's so much more to them than what we can easily see. We can hold these beliefs without really being aware that we have them; they just seem like the truth to us.

They might show up as beliefs about what is good or bad, right or wrong, and so on. They might show up in what we tolerate and what we find intolerable. They can be connected to our culture, our families of origin, or our social roles. They can feel small, like strong ideas about how to set a table, or huge, like beliefs about the moral importance of productivity or timeliness.

These organizing principles can cause us so much pain, especially if we aren't aware of them. We feel that something is wrong or that someone has wronged us, but we can't easily say why. Because they are held in our minds as objectively true (even though they aren't necessarily), when these principles are violated, we feel violated. These beliefs, these objects thrown together in this old trunk of hand-me-downs, are best held lightly.

I feel like a big part of the work of therapy is often sorting through this trunk, looking at each object, exploring our feelings about it, and then deciding what kind of relationship we want to have with it. We have choices, although it can be challenging and even painful to exercise those choices. Other people may not like it if we do.

I do believe the pain of carrying all of that with us, without awareness or intention, is greater than the pain associated with the conversations that happen when we exercise our choice and practice discernment. I see this as a process of coming into true adulthood, which is a moment that comes at different times for everyone (and some people might never get there). We look at our beliefs and our behaviours without judgment but with deep curiosity, and we decide what truly serves us and helps us become the people we want to be.

When I was working through this with a friend, she asked, "What's the difference between an organizing principle and a value?" I think for the purposes of the work that we're doing together here, values are what we're left with when we sort through our trunk of hand-me-downs and decide what we're going to keep. I'm making it sound like it's easy to identify our values—it may or may not be—but there are processes that can help us sort out what resonates for us and what does not.

We can start by asking these questions: Who and what matters most to me? What do I value?

It seems to work best when we start with *who*. Humans are

relational creatures, and it helps us clarify our values when we identify the other stars in our particular constellation. Who do we love, what values do we want to demonstrate to them, and who do we trust? Who represents connection and community to us?

Then we can move to *what*. We don't need to identify goals here, although goals often show up. We are trying to understand the *why* attached to the goal. We want money? That's nice. Why? Maybe we crave financial stability because we've experienced the destructive impact of poverty. Maybe we associate money with power, which then opens up the question of why we want power. We need to know what and why before we start making decisions and committing to action.

It's easy to fall into self-criticism during this process, and so we can take a breath if we find that we're telling ourselves we should or shouldn't care about something. What we're doing here is noticing—just noticing. We want to name what is important to us without judgment, as though we are reading the names of books off a shelf. We are not concerned right now with good/bad or right/wrong, or what we should or shouldn't want or feel. We need to see what's there. At different points in our lives we may notice some values getting louder and others getting quieter, and that's okay.

We will know we're headed in the right direction if the things that show up here are centred around our values and our experiences. When we start listing things like "It's important to me that my children are well behaved" or "It's important that my colleagues show me respect," it might be good to hit pause and rework these thoughts a little. A cause of so much human sadness, loneliness, and frustration is locating our wellbeing in someone else's response to us. We so often look for our sense of safety, of identity, in other people, but we will never find it there. We can't be in balance if we depend on someone else's opinion to feel fulfilled.

We might want to live in a way that encourages others to feel respect for us—that might be achievable. But ultimately, it's the other person's job to feel and think whatever they're going to feel and think, and we cannot do that work for them.

We can also cause ourselves a lot of pain by having strong feelings about our values being shared. Of course, if something is important to us, we will want others to care about it too! Of course, if something grounds us or brings us joy, we'll want others to experience that as well. If we think back to our image of hand-me-downs, there might be something in our trunk that we find so delightful and wonderful that we can't imagine someone else not wanting it. We might try to give this wonderful object to someone else, and if they have a negative response to it we might feel angry or sad. Those feelings get to be there; they aren't the enemy, and they also aren't an invitation to force or ask someone else to take responsibility for them.

There is a limit to what we can do to influence other people's values and choices, just like our power to dictate what someone does with a gift we give them is limited. Pushing hard usually is met with a pushing away. The most we can do (which is a lot and can absolutely make a difference) is live our values, openly and authentically. We can share them, and we can model them.

When I find myself frustrated because someone else isn't understanding the importance of a value that matters to me, I either silently or sometimes out loud add "For me" at the beginning of a values statement. This sounds something like, "For me, it's really important to be on time." Or: "For me, it really matters to hand everything in by the deadline." It helps remind me that (a) this gets to be important to me and (b) I should not assume this is a shared value.

This mirrors what happens if I give someone a gift I think is really great, and the recipient doesn't like it. I remind myself that I had the privilege of experiencing or using something and deciding if it was useful to me or not, and now the *real* gift I'm giving to this person is the chance to go through the same process.

When we start to clarify and articulate our values and when we let go of the idea that we can impose our values on others, we might find ourselves experiencing real disconnection from people in our lives or even whole communities. Someone who occupies a place of friend or loved one in our life might hold values that are very opposed to ours. In some instances, these differing values can live next door to one another comfortably enough. In others, we realize that there is not actually room for compromise. James Baldwin said it perfectly: "We can disagree and still love each other unless your disagreement is rooted in my oppression and denial of my humanity and right to exist."

Big values might show up here; we might say that we value reliability and kindness, or creativity and generosity. We might also notice that we feel best in nature or in a busy city, or that when we're very stressed we love reading murder mysteries. All of these things can matter; these big and little pieces can come together to form a person we both genuinely are and would really like to be.

How can you identify what your values are? Some people like to write out how they'd like to be introduced at an imaginary awards ceremony when they win a lifetime achievement award—what qualities would the speaker name? Others think about what they'd want written in their obituary. I don't think it's possible to get this wrong, if we give ourselves some space to think about what's genuinely important to us. Jot down five or six thoughts, and start experimenting with those. If these thoughts ground us and help us identify what moves we want to make, then we're on the right track . . . and if we're ever feeling lost, we can open up the trunk and remind ourselves of what's in there, of who we are and who we are choosing to be.

As is the case with many of the images included in this book, this one has acquired many layers and embellishments courtesy of various people over the years. That's one of the loveliest things about this work—seeing what others do with the first image and what amazing processes they build on top of it. One client imagined herself as the proprietor of a fabulous antique shop full of magical things. Her job, when someone brought in a box of objects to sell to her, was to spread them out on her counter and look at them very carefully. It was not only her choice but really her responsibility to take her time; she also realized she could take all, some, or nothing from the box. The final layer for her was realizing that even if she had accepted something before, it was (and is) always in her power to get rid of it if her understanding of its value to her had changed.

Another client envisioned himself at an all-you-can-eat buffet. He felt (and I have to agree) that the best way of approaching a buffet is to check the whole thing out first so you don't accidentally fill yourself up with something like bread and miss the most delicious thing that you really want that's further down the table. I also appreciated his description of getting to go back for a second round with a clean plate; that layered a theme of freedom onto our discussion.

What all of these images give us is some space and grace so that we can look, think, choose, revisit, and choose again. They bring the process of choosing into the centre, they allow us to take the time that we need, and they free us from the weight of regret because we can always go back with a clean plate and choose again.

Try this

Let's go through this trunk together. What are some hand-me-downs that you've been given by your family? Your culture? Your friends?

Feeling stuck? We can sort the contents of the trunk into two groups. Self-related organizing principles are about our own worth, lovability, or competence. Other-related principles or beliefs are about how the world is supposed to work and how we see other people.

What do you believe to be true about yourself? What do you think is true about the world or about other people? Write down a few examples. Then ask yourself *Is this always true?* Do any counter-narratives show up . . . stories of moments when these beliefs were not true? If you look back—way back, in your own life—can you remember the first time you encountered this organizing principle? Do you remember who told you it was true?

When you've got a bit of a list, take a moment to read through it and notice what you're feeling as you do so. Which principles feel precious? Which beliefs have harmed you? Which ones feel like clutter?

Imagine a dry erase board

Let's keep playing with organizing principles and values. A big part of identifying and working with them is understanding the huge impact our environment can have on our capacity to connect with our values in any given moment and appreciating that any moments of disconnection are impermanent, though they may not feel like that when we're in the middle of them.

When I worked in the hospital doing family support, my job was to help parents with babies in the NICU. Even if you've never been in an NICU, I bet you can still appreciate what a difficult time it is for families (and if you have been in an NICU, I'm sending you a huge hug right now). It was the most meaningful, the most wonderful, and the most challenging job I've ever had.

I remember having a conversation with a new mother who said, "Nothing about this experience matches what I thought I would be like as a mom. I thought I'd be an easygoing hippie mom, all about rolling in the mud and taking my baby backpacking, and here I am weighing diapers and tracking every drop my baby eats!" She waved with disgust at a dry erase board near her baby's incubator that had a table drawn on it for tracking various data points related to her baby. To be clear: those dry-erase boards had a vital function, that data was really important, and the board itself was a great tool for transparent communication. It's just that she had never imagined that she'd be in a position where this would be necessary.

At the time I commiserated with her, and I don't really remember what I shared in return, but her words stuck with me. I realized much later that she had identified something really challenging that happens in places like NICUs. I think you might see some of the same processes at work in other institutions—I've certainly had similar experiences in school or some workplaces, and even in some relationships.

You come in with your set of beliefs and hopes about who you're going to be and what you're going to do. Right now, I'm imagining you writing them down on a dry-erase board with a vivid marker, perhaps making a nice long list of your values and hopes. Everything you write down is important to you. Then someone comes in with a big eraser and just cleans that board right off. They replace everything you wrote with something else, and you get the overwhelming feeling that while you're in that place, you'll have to fall in line with what's on that board. How you sound, what you say, what you look like, what you do—you may feel you've been told very clearly what's acceptable and what is not.

That may in fact be true, in that place and in that moment. There are some spaces in which we don't have any choices, where we don't feel heard or seen or understood, and these are not psychologically safe spaces for anyone. Marsha Linehan, the originator of Dialectical Behavioural Therapy, described these sorts of spaces as "invalidating environments" in which we have the feeling of not belonging, as if our essential self is somehow not welcomed or appreciated.

What's more, any expression of "negative" or difficult emotion is discouraged, and any complex feeling we do try to express is perceived as a moral failing or character flaw on our part. The people who maintain these invalidating environments may or may not have any conscious awareness of what they're doing, which can exacerbate the pain we experience. We are made to feel like the problems and limitations of the system we're stuck in are caused by our mistakes or flaws, and so we are assigned blame for any harm that we experience. You can see this play out on so many levels of our society, where we blame individuals for the failings of our systems. To be stuck in an invalidating environment with no hope of escape, with no chance to engage with our own values in daily life, is destructive to a person on every level.

When we notice that we're in one of these invalidating environments, perhaps the most protective thing we can do is hold onto our hope. We may have to fight hard to do this, but can we remember that these rules we're being made to follow are not chiselled in stone—they're scribbled on a dry-erase board? Can we believe that some day (hopefully soon), we'll get to hold the eraser?

It seems like a fact of modern life that we often have to spend some time in environments where we don't have control of the marker or eraser, and it's unlikely that these spaces are going to change (at least not in the short term). In those situations, it is important to have access to restorative places and communities, where we can assert and celebrate our own values and experiences. Those restorative moments will help protect our value systems from being warped or damaged, and they will remind us of who we really are.

It may also be true that when we do get to hold the eraser, we may choose to keep something that someone else wrote down. Both my children spent quite some time in the NICU when they were born, and there were many things I learned from some beloved nurses and doctors that I chose to keep long after we left the hospital. There were other beliefs and behaviours I held onto for many years, until I eventually decided they didn't serve me or my family. And guess what? I still had the eraser! Over the years other people have added to my board—writers, friends, teachers, clients, family members—and somehow I always find space.

We may also find that there are seasons or moments when a particular set of rules, values, or practices serves us well, and then we move into another season and they no longer work. Ideally, we develop a habit of checking in on our list, revisiting our dry-erase board, so that we don't labour under the weight of outdated rules for too long. For example, I'm thinking of how when my kids were little, we followed a very specific nap schedule for a time because it worked so perfectly. I was so sad when they grew out of it, but at least I recognized it was time to let it go. Imagine if I'd grimly hung onto it because THOSE WERE THE RULES? Dragging eight-year-olds out of playdates because it was nap time or trying to tuck fourteen-year-olds in at 2 p.m.? It sounds absurd, and yet we do things like this all the time, simply because "that's the way we've always done it." It can be scary to erase some of these rules, to let go of something that felt protective or created order, but if something is genuinely serving us, of course, it can stay. We just want to create opportunities to check what's written on our board and see what answers surface when we ask ourselves *Why is this here*?

Now I'm imagining that lovely mother from a decade ago. I spoke to her a couple of years ago, and it was beautifully and hilariously clear that she did in fact take an eraser to all those rigid rules and particular procedures, and she replaced them with some glorious words about adventure and laughter and flexibility and fun and mess.

Let me share something else that came from a parent in a hospital support group. We were working with this metaphor, and one parent said that he felt his list had been written in permanent marker and he was never going to get rid of it. We took a moment to acknowledge his worry and sadness, and then another participant got the most gleeful look on her face. She said, "I am honestly not making this up, but to get permanent marker off of the board, you draw over it again and again with a dry-erase marker! It works!"

We laughed together about how great this expansion on our initial metaphor was, that perhaps the only way to deal with something that feels permanent is to go over and over it again with what you choose, until only smudges remain. Doesn't something about that feel so right?

Try this

Take a moment to think about an environment you spend a lot of time in. It might be work or school or a family system. What are the rules associated with that environment? Imagine them written on your dry-erase board.

Do you know where these rules came from? How do they make you feel about yourself? Are they your rules or someone else's? Who put them there? Are they helpful to you?

Can you feel that eraser in your hand?

Imagine cars going
down the street

We can have a very solid sense of our values, of who and what is important to us, and we can have a similarly strong understanding of what our organizing principles are and how they got there. And even with all of that wisdom, we can find ourselves wide awake at 2 a.m., watching thought after thought cross our minds, and feeling tormented by helplessness or misery or fear. It's almost like we're being attacked by our thoughts and emotions in those moments. We switch positions, we try to distract ourselves—we will do just about anything to banish those thoughts from our minds, but they keep marching in.

That happens because we don't have control over our thoughts and feelings. They are events, they happen, they have a beginning, a middle, and an end. We have no more control over our thoughts or emotions than we do over the weather. When we tangle with thoughts and feelings in an attempt to control or erase them, we end up causing ourselves pain. This is, according to some philosophies and religions, actually the main source of our pain.

This isn't something that people like to hear. They say things like "But I can't bear these thoughts! Please help me stop thinking them! I don't want to think of myself like this—make it go away! I can't endure this feeling—make it stop!" And I wish with my whole heart, for my sake as well as theirs, that I could help them banish those thoughts they don't want to think and erase those feelings they don't want to feel. But I can't.

Instead, I often turn to a metaphor I first encountered when I was learning about Acceptance Commitment Therapy (ACT). I might ask someone to imagine a street. Maybe it's their own street, if they live on a street.

"Do you have control over the cars that drive down your street?" I ask. They often laugh.

"Nope! Wish I did . . . but no."

"Do you have control over who parks close to your home?" Again, they respond with a no.

"Do you have control over who might get out of their car and ring your doorbell or buzz your apartment?"

"No."

And then we make the connection between those cars, the people in them, and our thoughts and related feelings. We have no more control over our thoughts than we do over the cars driving down the street. Sometimes if a thought is very persistent and hangs around (like a parked car), we start wondering if it is somehow more significant than the other thoughts that come and go, but it's still not something we have control over. And when that thought gets really, really loud, like when a car alarm goes off, or if someone gets out of the car and comes up to our door and knocks, we might start thinking it's significant, that there must be some meaning to it. We might notice a big feeling connected to that thought. And yet all we know about it at this point is that it's a thought that has shown up.

Once when I was exploring this metaphor in a support group, one participant shouted, "It's just like shoe shopping online!" We laughed and waited for some clarification.

She said, "When you look at a pair of shoes, and you really like them, but then you realize they're way too expensive. But then EVERYWHERE you go online you see some ad for those shoes, and it starts feeling like you're meant to buy them! Like it's meaningful that you're always seeing the shoes? And so you end up buying them . . . but it's not because there's any meaning in it. It's just the algorithm!"

We all gasped with recognition. The more often a thought shows up, the more we assign significance to it—but it's just the algorithm doing its thing. It's just a car doing its thing, driving down a street.

At what point do we have control over our thoughts? I don't think the word "control" is particularly useful here, so let's think about what kind of *relationship* we want to have with a thought. We can start by giving the thought a name. This helps create a bit of distance between ourselves and our thoughts, and that distance can feel like relief.

One way of doing this is to say, when we notice a challenging or persistent thought showing up, "I'm having a thought that _____" (and then describe the thought). If we would like even more distance, we can say, "I'm noticing that I'm having a thought that _____." I first encountered this technique when reading the wonderful work of Russ Harris, and it does a great job of creating a bit of space for some curiosity to come in and interrupt the internal thought tango that can be so difficult. In practice, it sounds something like: "I'm such a bad person." "I'm having a thought that I'm a bad person." "I'm noticing that I'm having a thought that I'm a bad person." See how much room opens up?

Let's look at a situation, a really painful situation, and think about how this technique might help us in such a moment. Something I'm not a fan of is "positive thinking," which sounds like a strange thing to say. What's wrong with thinking positive thoughts? Nothing—unless you blame yourself (or criticize other people) for other kinds of thoughts that show up. The idea that only positive thoughts are welcome causes great harm, especially to those who are trapped in tough situations.

I remember one mother in a support group bravely naming her fear out loud that her baby might not make it home, which is a reasonable thing to fear when your baby is hospitalized and very sick. Another mother jumped in telling her she wasn't allowed to say or think that because it would hurt her baby. I gently intervened at that moment to make space for those difficult thoughts and to help the group members recognize that these were just thoughts; they weren't facts, and they weren't going to make anything happen. The thought is not the enemy. It's a car driving down the street. And sometimes we're in a place or a moment where we're going to hear many, many cars driving down the street. So, to name the thought out loud, to figure out how to hold it so that we can do what we want to do and be who we want to be, even with that loud, distracting car driving up and down the street, is wise and brave, and it's the first step toward thinking and feeling a bit differently.

We tried that distancing technique in that moment. "I'm noticing that I'm having a thought that my baby is so sick and might not come home from the hospital." That led to "I love her so much, and I am so tired, and I feel so alone and afraid." That led to a supportive discussion in community, which led to "I'm going to go show her how much I love her with a good long cuddle, and then I'm going to call my mom." Notice that we didn't spend a lot of time tangling with the original thought. It was named, and then our attention moved to the feelings behind the thought, and then to what she could do that might feel important. She couldn't erase her fear or worry, and that wasn't the goal. The goal was to help her carry it in a way that allowed her to open up to a different experience, one that didn't feel so hopeless.

Opening ourselves up to a different experience is part of what we're trying to do when we name our thoughts as cars or algorithms. We are cultivating our ability to move between our experiencing self and our noticing or observing self. This type of flexibility is often something we achieve after the fact; I'm sure we can all think of moments when we reacted in a particular way, and then minutes or months later realized we could have done something else. I think that with compassionate practice we can bring this awareness forward in our timeline, right into the present moment. It's like what that mom did in our group—she brought her awareness into the now and gave herself room to try something different.

It starts with valuing the importance of both stances. The experiencing self is so important; it's the part that really enjoys the delicious orange and gets lost in the mesmerizing music. It's the part that gets knocked down by big grief and lifted up by big joy. The observing self also matters. It's the part of us that sees other people, puts things into context, creates stories, and finds meaning. Some of our suffering arises when we get stuck in one stance. We cannot enjoy the beautiful music because we can't shift away from noticing and contextualizing and storytelling, or we can't support a loved one because we're trapped in our own immediate experience.

Questions I sometimes ask myself, if I'm wondering if I'm stuck in a particular stance, are *What is the work of this moment? Is there something to experience, or is there something to notice?* We can shift between stances in a nanosecond; the question serves as an invitation, not a criticism. If I ask myself what my stance is, it gives me an opportunity to identify if I'm stuck in a ruminating cycle, which is a deeply human thing to do but not perhaps how I really want to be spending my time. Once I notice what I'm doing, it gives me a chance to interrupt the process. I can name the cars, I can name the algorithm, and I can decide what I want to try next.

Imagining cars may not be for you, and you might hate the idea of thinking about online shopping and algorithms—and that's fine!

Let's turn to the sky instead. Sky gazing is a core practice of the Dzogchen school of Tibetan Buddhism. Looking at the sky helps us connect with thoughts about what is temporary, what is permanent, and what is beautiful. It can help us find a way to see our thinking and hold our suffering, not to erase it but to hold it.

When applying therapeutic models like Dialectical Behavioural Therapy or Acceptance Commitment Therapy to this practice, we might first envision the sky and then notice the clouds that cross it or the snow that falls from it. We might name the sky as our own self and the clouds or the weather as our thoughts or emotions or our daily experiences. The sky is always there. The clouds, the rain, the wind, and the snow come and go. And as we noted before, we cannot control the weather, and we cannot govern the clouds. The rain needs to come and go, and the wind needs to move—just like how our emotions need to move. The sky cannot be destroyed by the weather; it has endless capacity to hold whatever weather shows up.

In my hardest moments, turning to the sky has been deeply grounding. There are some moments that are dramatically beautiful, like a gentle sunrise, a vivid sunset, or an uninterrupted expanse of blue. But what I've come to appreciate is that the sky is always beautiful, in grey or blue or sunshine or snow or day or night. It is always varied, always moving, and always changing. It is always there, and if I'm feeling shaky, I can always turn to it to be reminded of its permanence.

Try this

Let's practice naming and noticing our thoughts. You can look out a window at a nearby street and focus on cars driving by, or you can look up at the sky. Pick out a car or a cloud and identify it as a thought. "That blue truck is me thinking I'm not good enough" or "That dark cloud is me feeling so angry with my parents."

You may then notice that you have no control about what happens next. The thought might drive itself right out of your field of vision or float away across the sky. It might stop right at the corner or merge with another cloud.

Does externalizing that thought and pinning it onto this outside object change how you feel about it? What does it feel like when another thought pulls up or drifts by? Do you notice your relationship to your thought changing?

Imagine a container

If we can't get rid of our thoughts, what do we do if we find ourselves stuck in rumination? What if our thoughts feel particularly challenging or intrusive? Have you ever had this happen at night, when you're desperate to get to sleep, and suddenly your most embarrassing moments start playing on a hideous loop? Or perhaps you start thinking about choices you regret or things you said or mistakes you made. Or more tedious but still terrible, your to-do list starts unspooling, and you can't seem to make it stop. Unfettered, our imagination can exacerbate this mental mess, but if we use a visualization to give ourselves a framework we can use to engage it, that same imagination can bring us some relief.

I first encountered this container visualization when I was undergoing training for a type of therapy called EMDR (Eye Movement Desensitization and Reprocessing). Francine Shapiro developed protocols for this fascinating therapeutic model in 1987, although it has roots in and owes a deep debt to Indigenous practices that use movement, dance, and music to promote healing. If you've experienced trauma and are feeling stuck with it or in it, EMDR might be a good therapy for you to investigate.

I loved my EMDR training because it was so much more than what I had expected. I had anticipated something highly technical and focused on the bilateral movements that the therapy is known for. Instead, we spent hours discussing "resourcing," which in this context meant building safe relationships, developing self-care practices, and cultivating a deep awareness of and respect for our own states. We used rich imagery to help us stay with difficult moments and memories.

One example of this is the EMDR container. Before beginning the deep work of processing, an EMDR therapist will often help clients develop a container to hold thoughts and memories that are important but can't be processed in a particular moment. Once identified, the container is available whenever we need it to help us hold whatever may be feeling painful or stressful.

Though we're not doing EMDR together right now, let's see what it feels like to create a container. The most important thing for you to know is that there is no right or wrong with this; whatever comes to mind and whatever feels right for you is what matters.

So, if I ask you to imagine a container, what comes up for you? It could be pragmatic or prosaic. For example, my container is a laundry basket. Yours could be an intricately decorated box, a glowing glass bottle, or a giant bank vault. It could be something from your childhood home or something you use every day. Ideally, your container will have a lid or a door or a way of closing it up, so that whatever is inside can be kept safe.

When you close your eyes, what container do you see?

Perfect! Now that we've identified your container, let's imagine what it feels like to put thoughts or feelings inside it. I sometimes do this if something is nagging at me right when I want to go to bed. I imagine these thoughts as clothing items that I'm picking off the floor. I gently fold them up, one by one, and throw them into my hamper.

In my mind I name each item as I toss it as something that is worrying me, and I visualize the lid closing when I'm done. I know all those thoughts and worries will be held safe there, waiting until I'm ready to think about them again.

What do your thoughts look like? Are they bubbles that float into the container one by one? Are they scraps of coloured paper with words scribbled on them? Are they books that you're putting on a shelf, which will then be safely locked behind glass doors? Again, there's no right or wrong here. There is just a question. If you imagine your thoughts having a physical form, what comes up for you? And how would your thoughts make their way into your container?

Now you have a container, and you have an image for your thoughts, and you have a process for putting your thoughts safely into your container. What next?

We can imagine where this container is going to be kept. Is it in your home, in an imaginary place, or a place that is dear to you but far away? Think of a place that represents safety to you. That might be a good place to keep your container. What helps keep it safe there? Do you want to put a lock on the door, a moat around the castle, or turn on a highly sophisticated alarm system?

And finally, imagine a protector. Is there someone (real or imaginary) whom you trust to look after your container? Sometimes people put an old pet or stuffed animal in charge. Sometimes it's a beloved grandparent or the main character of your favourite book. This can be painful if we have had experiences of betrayal or rejection, so we can get creative here. In one session, a client felt very stuck for a while and then blurted out "Emma Thompson" in ringing tones, and we both realized Emma Thompson is a FANTASTIC container protector. (Two other celebrities who are often invoked—I doubt you'll be surprised by either—are Angela Bassett and The Rock.)

Now comes the fun part. Often, we talk about tools or skills to help us in hard times, but we don't try to use them until the hard moment is upon us. We don't usually think about practicing with these images or using these skills in calmer moments, because why would we when we're not in distress?

My invitation to you is to practice putting thoughts into your container regularly. You can integrate it into the close-down of your workday or into your nighttime ritual. You can test it out by calling on a slightly stressful memory and then seeing what it feels like to tuck that memory gently into your container. The more you practice, the more access you will have to this new skill when you're in a genuinely difficult moment. Expecting ourselves to execute a new skill perfectly the first time when we're under a huge amount of stress isn't fair, and it's not something we would do in other circumstances. Imagine an athlete being sent to the Olympics without ever practicing?

I find this container visualization especially effective if I'm dealing with heavy work stress; it helps me turn my attention to other parts of my life that deserve my attention and focus. It also helps if I'm struggling with an interpersonal situation (like a conflict with someone I care about) that can't be solved in the moment. I bring out my container, fold all my thoughts into my hamper, and my internal tension thermostat goes down a couple of degrees. I no longer feel the urge to "fix this now," which is so often unworkable and unproductive. My container gives me space, time, and perspective. Maybe yours could do the same for you?

Try this

Art therapists have an amazing ability to work with metaphor and make it tangible in the room. There's something about taking an idea out of your head and then using materials to make it something you can touch that's deeply powerful. So, if we approach this container metaphor using an art therapy lens, what could that look like?

The concept of the worry box is often used with kids, but I think it works beautifully for anyone of any age. You can decorate a box or a big envelope, and then you can decide how to represent your worries or challenging thoughts. You could write them down on slips of paper or draw small pictures of them and then place them inside the container. Next, decide how you're going to close and store your worry box. It can be interesting to go back after a week or a month to revisit those worries and notice if they still feel the same. Often, people notice that what used to feel like a terrible worry has either solved itself or softened somewhat.

Imagine a school bus

Let's think about what's happening when we say something like "A part of me wants to and another part of me doesn't." That's a really common thing to say and hear, and it's an acknowledgement that there are parts of ourselves that feel and think different things. We might notice some parts showing up when we have to go to work and other parts showing up when we go home to visit a family member. Many people (myself included) notice childish parts of themselves surfacing when they go back to their home town or reconnect with childhood friends. In some ways, this can be enjoyable and in other ways surprising or confusing.

There's a beautiful model of therapy called Internal Family Systems that takes this idea and really runs with it. Richard Schwartz, who developed the Internal Family Systems model, categorized different parts into three main groups: managers, firefighters, and exiles. When I think of a manager, I think of a Mary Poppins type of figure, who bustles in and makes sure everyone's fed and tucks us all into bed even if we're not tired. Managers keep things running and work hard to keep any troubling parts of the self quiet. Firefighters show up when we are (or perceive that we are) in danger. They can be helpful and encourage us to relax and enjoy ourselves, or they can cause harm by spurring us toward extreme behaviour to relieve our pain. Exiles are sometimes the youngest and the wisest parts; they are vulnerable and easily wounded. They are the parts we are often eager to disavow or move past. We associate these parts with shame and rejection.

In his wonderful book *No Bad Parts*, Schwartz makes it very clear that every part of us is worthy of love, has an important job to do, and needs to be included. Even the ones that feel embarrassing or confusing—perhaps especially those parts!

When this concept first started to resonate with me, I thought of a clown car, stuffed full of all the different parts of me. Younger, older, angry, officious, organized, goofy—I imagined a door popping open and all of these parts spilling out.

I then remembered another metaphor from Acceptance Commitment Therapy: the Passengers on the Bus. Steven Hayes created the exercise to help people understand how our internal experiences become passengers on our bus and influence how we drive. If you're the bus driver and you listen to your passengers (who represent your emotions and thoughts), and you do what they tell you instead of following your route, you might not get to where you want or need to go. The intent of this metaphor is to help us stay connected to our sense of what's most important (our destination) and disengage from distracting and temporary thoughts and feelings.

What happens when we bring these two ways of thinking together? Let's imagine a school bus. You are the driver—"you" being your integrated, or aware, self. You look at the passengers on your bus and recognize that they are all different parts of you. A five-year-old you might be on the bus sitting across the aisle from your snarky fifteen-year-old self. There might be an upset you, an afraid you, an organized you. There might be parts of you that you are proud of—a high achiever, a reliable worker, a good friend. There will also be parts that make you really uncomfortable—a dishonest part, a disloyal part, an unkind part, a whiny part, a mean part, a rageful part. All of these parts get to be there. All of these parts deserve love, attention, and to be known. No part gets left behind.

Now you're driving your bus with all of these parts on board. What happens next? Maybe they're all yelling! They're telling you to do different things. The five-year-old part is kicking the seat and singing, the fifteen-year-old part thinks the bus is stupid, the angry part is screaming at you to go faster, a manager is criticizing you, a firefighter is asking you to pull over and go drinking, and the parts you've tried to push away are whispering some really awful things at you, telling you to do something terrible.

None of this is easy, but there is one piece that's simple. It's up to you to drive the bus. It's not the job of the angry part or the reliable worker, and it is certainly not up to the five-year-old. It's okay for them to be there, and it's okay for them to have and share thoughts about how you're driving. But if you notice the five-year-old trying to grab the steering wheel, give yourself the gift of a pause and a breath, and remember that you are calm, you are confident, you are kind, and you are the driver.

Try this

Think about an internal conflict you may have been experiencing recently—a situation in which different parts of you want different things. Can you identify which parts of you are engaged? Is there a young part that wants fun, a managing part that is trying to avoid conflict, another part that thinks you're being an idiot and should just get on with things? What job is each part trying to do for you? What does it feel like to give each part a moment to have their say and then to make a decision from the perspective of your integrated self?

Imagine a stable
full of horses

Now that you've named and gotten to know some of these different parts of yourself, let's imagine that we're in a stable. There are beautiful horses in each stall, and all of these horses love to run, move about, and be around other horses.

Each horse represents a different part of you. Some are sturdy workhorses that come out every day. Some might be a bit more fragile or particular, and these horses come out to run only when the conditions are just right.

And then we have a third kind. These horses never get to run. They might be kind of challenging or inconvenient to deal with. Over time, you might see them doing things to themselves to distract from their loneliness or boredom, and these things might cause them harm. If they rarely get to come out, they might respond weirdly to an infrequent opportunity. They might not run as well as they used to, and you might be embarrassed or irritated about this.

In some cases, they've been shut up in the stable for so long it may seem like they've forgotten that there's another way to be or that there's a beautiful pasture waiting for them. In other cases, their frustration might build to a point where they just kick down the gates or jump over the fences and leave destruction in their wake. When we talk about mid-life crises, this is what comes to my mind—I see an image of a stable door that's been blown apart and no sign whatsoever of the escaping horse, who's now off and running.

Let's spend some time getting to know these lonely horses. What parts of you do they represent? If I asked you if there was a part of you that was longing to escape and run and play, what would come up for you?

Sometimes when I'm talking with parents or people who are approaching retirement, I notice certain patterns in their answers. People in these situations often identify whole parts of life that they miss. They long for adventure or for uncomplicated silliness. They miss being creative or having time to do things that aren't directly attached to a goal or an agenda. They feel like they're always playing it safe, and they wonder if any part of them is still brave enough to take some risks.

Often, people are afraid to name the longing because they think that if they name it, it will get louder, and they don't want to have to deal with it. There's no room in their life right now for anything other than what they're already doing, so it feels safer to keep ignoring that horse.

This is where I think it's useful to take a middle-path approach.

If we ignore those horses, at some point they will either harm them-selves or make a break for it, and then where will we be? What is our alternative?

Can we be kind to these horses? Can we be respectful of their needs and their pain? What would it look like to give them opportu-nities to run? What would it look like if we cared for these challeng-ing, complicated, pain-in-the-butt horses just as lovingly as we do our prize-winners?

As I read these words over to myself I feel really overwhelmed. That sounds like a lot of work. How can we get to know all these dif-ferent horses, all these different parts of self, and then take care of all of this when there is so much that we have to do all the time? It feels impossible. In a moment I'll introduce you to a lovely tool that's going to help you find your way through this. For now, I'll share something that a dear friend told me a long time ago that felt true at the time and feels increasingly true as I get older.

She was my mother's age, and after my mom died, she often stepped in very kindly when I needed guidance. At that time, I felt frozen and unsure of what direction to go in because I was afraid that any commitment I made to something meant cutting off other possibilities. In a way, I wasn't letting any horses run because I couldn't decide who should go first.

I remember her saying to me, "We've done a terrible disservice to young people, telling them that they can have it all but not tell-ing them how. The truth is that there is so much room in your life to have some version of whatever you want, but you can't have it all at the same time. Pick something to try, go for it, see what happens, and then try something else. You're not in a hurry."

Those words felt like relief in my twenties, and now that I'm in my fifties and on my third or fourth career, they feel like permission or excitement. There is no rush. Every part of yourself can have its turn. Every horse will get a chance to run. I just have to keep paying attention.

Try this

Clients often ask what paying attention looks like. How do we keep track of our horses? This is where I turn to a lovely tool originally developed by psychologist Tobias Lundgren, called the Bull's Eye Diagram.

First, draw a circular bull's-eye or target with four or five rings. Draw lines across the middle to divide it into four quarters. Label each quarter as a domain of life that matters to you. You could try Work/Education, Relationships/ Family, Fun/Leisure, and Personal Growth/Health. If there are other categories that are important to you, feel free to add them, but don't have more than six segments. Rank the segments in order of most to least important. By saying something is least important, we're not saying it doesn't matter! We're just saying it's the least important right now. Not everything can be the most important thing at once.

Next, think about what you do over the course of a week. Do your actions reflect how important each category is? No judgment here. Just noticing.

If you think you're really living according to your values in a particular domain, put an X close to the centre of the bull's-eye. If you notice that your actions aren't lining up with the importance of that domain, so you're not really living according to your values, put an X further out from the centre.

If a domain isn't of top importance to you, now might not be the moment to worry about it. It might just be something to keep paying attention to. If a domain is very important to you, and you're not close to the centre, treat it as a call to action. What can you do over the next week related to this area of life?

Imagine a dog

Do you have friends who communicate with you via internet memes and videos? It might be the only thing preventing me from completely cutting the social media cord—seeing these snippets of ridiculousness and wonder. A dear friend just sent me a video of her favourite thing, which is dogs doing agility training. She loves seeing the dogs zip around the courses, and the delight they seem to take in executing each trick. After watching a particularly lovely video featuring a basset hound, we talked about why these videos are so satisfying.

She said, "I can relate to how happy they are when they complete their circuit. I kind of get the same feeling when I get to the end of a long day, and I've ticked off every task. Everyone fed! Got everyone where they needed to be when they needed to be there! Errands done! Job done. Meetings endured. Took my vitamins, called my mother, made dinner, prepped for tomorrow. Done, done, done."

Then a pause. "The main difference is that the dogs get to stop. And they get a treat at the end."

In that moment, we laughed and laughed—but there's a painful piece here too. It can be really satisfying to hack through our days, to line up our tasks and knock them off one by one, like a pool shark or a dog racing through an agility course. There are entire industries devoted to helping us bring this kind of precision and efficiency to our days. We can buy products and hire consultants and take courses and fill out templates so that we can execute more, do more, and layer on more obstacles to conquer in the spaces we open up.

The problem with this is that dogs need rest. We need rest.

There are loud messages in our culture right now that we should be productive, should plan, should grind, should take on side gigs, should multitask while we multitask. We should fill up every corner of our lives with productivity and work. The precarious economic reality that many people experience makes these messages even louder, and it would be disingenuous and insulting to pretend that the pressure isn't real and the need to work isn't there.

And yet—there's something I keep coming back to. Those dogs need to rest. And we do too.

How can we claim the rest that we need? First, I think we have to tell the truth about how liveable our lives are, as we've constructed them to be. Is our daily experience one of tension and stress as we strive to execute trick after trick, with no breaks or relief in between? Even if we notice satisfaction at the end of the day, can we also notice what we feel as the day rolls out? What are our bodies telling us? Is there tension in our jaw, our face, or our stomach? Do we feel sick at certain moments (like when we go into work or when we start our commute home), or are we more likely to get sharp in our language at particular times?

If our lives are packed so tightly that we're living in an activated state most of the time, that's not something we can meal plan, carpool, or batch cook our way out of. We may have to make tough decisions about asking for help or letting some things go. I say this knowing that these are incredibly difficult things to do. Asking for help makes us feel vulnerable, and there may not be people we feel we can ask for help. We might experience painful feelings about the family and friends we wish would be there to help but aren't. It may be a longer project to work toward, to build connections and community where support can be exchanged.

One of the greatest gifts we can give ourselves is community, because always doing things alone is exhausting and destructive. Our culture tells us a lot of stories about "self-made" successes, but all of those stories are lies. There are very few—perhaps no—true stories of people who did things all on their own. Whenever I hear one of those stories, I listen for the erasures. Whose contribution is being ignored? Who isn't being noticed or thanked for how they helped or what they did? If we turn back to our own story, what comes up for us when we think of asking for help? Is it a story of "I'm not enough" or "I'm not capable"? If we're measuring ourselves against false narratives of independence, we're always going to feel like we're not enough. We need to widen our personal and cultural stories to include and acknowledge all the helping hands that are part of any success, so that no one feels any shame when it's their turn for assistance.

Let's think back to those lovely dogs who have done such a great job mastering all their tricks. When they finish the course, they get treats, they get praise from their person, and then they get to play and rest—and maybe get a nice sniff-fest with their dog friends. What would it feel like if our days ended with treats, praise, connection, and rest? Would we approach the next day with energy and curiosity, instead of with the thought of *Oh no, here we go again*?

You may find it hard to let go of the idea of performing and doing because many people may depend on (or at least be very used to) you taking care of things. What I've found in my experiments with this is that claiming a bit of rest and space actually enhances relationships.

I recently saw another great video of a sheepdog herding sheep into a paddock, and something about it really stuck with me. I realized my brain often acts like that sheepdog, trying to herd my people in one direction or another or trying to anticipate what might be about to happen so that I can direct my people and myself away from it. I notice a defensive part of me showing up, trying to justify why I do that. I want things to go well! I don't want things to be difficult if they don't have to be. I don't want my loved ones to suffer!

This image resonates for many clients who are exhausted by the constant running but aren't quite sure how to stop. There's a fear there. What happens if we take a break from running after the sheep? Will one get lost or fall off the mountain? One trauma survivor shared that they feel more like a bomb-sniffing dog; their vigilance had kept them alive for so long, so the idea of relaxing is terrifying.

If I sit with these thoughts for a moment, I realize that those sheepdog tendencies probably don't serve my relationships very well. Nobody likes to be treated like a sheep. Nobody wants a bomb-sniffing dog constantly circulating around them. Sometimes they want to solve their problems in their own way—and sometimes their solutions are better!

It's also exhausting for us to be running constantly trying to get ahead of the problem, and to be thinking all the time about every permutation and combination of events and related consequences. These are hard realizations to sit with, so I want to move slowly and with compassion for myself and for others involved in the dynamic. There are certain habits I have that I think serve me well that I have no intention of getting rid of (like always bringing snacks on trips or having weekly overview discussions with my family so we all know what's happening when). Maybe my inner sheepdog can do one run round the meadow and then lie down in the shade for a bit, knowing that the sheep are just fine where they are.

Try this

Let's focus on rest for a moment. Our productivity-obsessed culture makes us feel so ashamed of wanting or needing rest, and yet it's so essential. In the magnificent book *Rest is Resistance: A Manifesto*, Tricia Hersey writes, "We must believe we are worthy of rest. We don't have to earn it. It is our birthright. It is one of our most ancient and primal needs."

So how are you going to meet this need? What can come off your plate? What can you say no to? Can you be slightly less available in certain areas of your life? Put your phone on do not disturb. Take a whole day off from looking at messages. Lie on your floor or your sofa for 10 minutes and look at the ceiling. See what it feels like to not have to rush, to not have to do. If you can't find the time to try any of these moves, treat that as a warning signal. If we don't make time for rest, our bodies will claim it for us in ways that might not be comfortable or convenient.

Claim your rest.

Imagine an air mattress

Think of a really good air mattress. It's strong but has a bit of give. If something falls on it, that thing will bounce a little but won't break. The mattress is comfortable and supports you well.

Now imagine that same air mattress with a little less air in it. It's a little less bouncy and much less comfortable. As air continues to leave the mattress (slowly, so that you might not even notice the change), in time you find yourself lying on a hard floor with nothing cushioning your body.

If we're thinking about you and your wellbeing and your day-to-day capacity, we could give that air mattress a few different names. It could be your zone of capacity or your window of tolerance, whichever you prefer. And the same thing that happens to the air mattress when it starts losing air happens to you when you experience too much pressure or when your air (both literal and figurative) starts escaping. Your zone of capacity starts getting thinner and thinner. Things don't bounce off you like they normally do.

Often people come into a session saying something like, "I have no idea why I have no energy," or "For some reason I've been crying all the time, and I don't understand," or "My fuse is so short these days, and I'm so ashamed of myself." When we explore a little, it usually comes out that they've been dealing with a lot around the clock. Pressure from different realms or arenas—work, family, relationships, racism, health, global events, discrimination, traumatic occurrences, economic injustice—all shows up and drains energy from the individual. Sometimes the pressure comes from something that we've called "good," like a promotion, parenting children, or attending a social event, but that still requires energy outflow. Usually about 50 percent of the pressure comes from meeting someone else's standards or fulfilling obligations that are only important to another person, and not necessarily to you.

So, if you're behaving in ways that don't feel like the you you're familiar with, treat that as a cue to ask yourself what has been calling on your energy lately. Why do you think your air mattress is deflating? Try to hold any judgment that comes up lightly. You might find yourself saying things like, "But helping my sister plan a party is fun. Why am I complaining about it?" Or, "Other people don't find studying so hard, so I shouldn't be struggling." In this moment we are just trying to notice what is, not what should or could be. Is something asking you to give it energy? If the answer is yes, it goes on the list. We're not making a list of things to get rid of; we're just making a list.

Once you make your list, you're often able to see just how

much you're carrying. You can see that there's the equivalent of an elephant jumping on your air mattress. There might even be a herd of elephants! It might start making sense to you, even on a physical level, why things are feeling hard. There's so much flowing from you that you can almost hear the air escaping.

At this point you can choose what to do next. You can look at ways to put air back in the mattress, you can think about what can come off of the air mattress, or you can do both.

What's the first thing that comes to mind when we think of putting air back into the mattress? If something related to breathing came up for you, you're not alone. That's usually what people say first, and it's a wise idea. Developing your own practice around breathing is a wonderful gift to the self, and there are so many possibilities out there to try. Simple is good. You can start with slow inhales and exhales through the nose. Breathwork has a long and rich history, and you can spend a lot of time exploring and learning various modalities; please be careful not to become distracted by the millions of possibilities available to you. It doesn't really matter which ones you try, and you're under no pressure to pick the "perfect" practice. What's most important is that you take a moment to try breathing slowly, in and out, and notice what happens next.

Breathwork is effective for many people, but if it's not working for you, that's okay! What else might fill up your mattress? This is where things might get more personal and more particular, and it's helpful to remember that there is no right or wrong there. There's what works for you and what doesn't. If everything on your first list could be roughly categorized as outflow (in that each item requires an outflow of energy from you to it), your next list will represent inflow. Everything you mention will give you something, like delight or rest or inspiration or joy or uncomplicated connection.

You can start by thinking about what appeals to your senses. What brings you a bit of delight? Reading a poem, smelling a beautiful aroma, sharing a joke with a friend, petting a dog, or stretching your body? If you can bring a genuine curiosity to this question and treat what shows up with respect (i.e., not belittling yourself for liking the smell of vanilla or enjoying the feeling of hugging a stuffed animal), you'll develop a wonderful toolbox that you can have with you always.

It can be a bit harder to think about what to take off of the air mattress, but this is often the essential piece. If we looked at every obligation we felt an attachment to, did an honest assessment of how much time each one would take, and added it all up, we would swiftly realize that what we had committed to was impossible.

This kind of reminds me when I was discharged from the hospital with my first child, who required various specialist appointments every week. We were incredibly grateful to have access to these clinicians and all the support they provided. But I began to feel a mounting sense of dread and inadequacy grow as one after another gave us lists of therapies and interventions we should be doing every day. At a certain point, I sat down with one of my daughter's physiotherapists, and we added up everything we'd been told to do—and it amounted to 11 hours of therapeutic intervention every day. I remember crying but then feeling a kind of relief, because it was so clearly not possible, so my failure no longer felt personal. Our wonderful physio then said, "Do what you can, but most important—have fun with her."

So that kind of thought might help us decide what stays and what goes. What's most important right now? What's fun right now? What's necessary right now? Is this a real need that's being met, or is it obligation? Is it something that matters to us or to someone else? Have we made something be big when it could be a bit smaller? We don't have to worry about next year or the year after that. We can centre ourselves in the present moment and think about what fits into our lives as they are today. If it pains us to think about getting rid of something, we can change the metaphor. We aren't throwing it away; we're putting it on ice for later.

It really comes down to physics, doesn't it? It's not a moral failing on the part of an air mattress if it needs more air. It's just science. It's just true. And the principle applies to you. If you're flat, and you've lost your bounce, it's not because you're lazy or selfish or unmotivated. You just need a little air.

Try this

Take a moment to list all the elephants dancing on your air mattress (or name all the items on your regular to-do list). This list represents Outflow.

Which ones are the most important to you?

Which ones are there because they're important for someone else?

Now take a moment and note everything on your Inflow list. What brings you energy? What helps you feel grounded? You can put big items on here but please also include small moves as well. You may not always have the resources or the time to go to a spa or on a trip, but there's almost always time for a cup of your favourite tea or to listen to your favourite song.

Imagine a medicine cabinet

Think of a time when you had a terrible headache. Maybe you staggered into your bathroom and opened the medicine cabinet, hoping that there would be something in there that hadn't expired. There might be one kind of pill that works fast but upsets your stomach. Hopefully, there's something in there that will help and not hurt. If you can't find anything, you might go to your room and close your eyes, placing a cold cloth over your forehead.

You might do something similar if you've pulled a muscle, or you could try seeking distraction with Netflix or YouTube or your favourite snack food.

This is a very human thing that people do. When we're in pain we seek relief. We're even willing to do something that causes us another type of harm if it addresses our big pain, and if we can't escape our pain directly, we'll opt for distraction. In some contexts, we feel fine about doing this and in others we feel shame. For example, no one would bat an eye if I took something to help with a headache, but medicating loneliness with alcohol would probably prompt a different response.

Before we define what is and what isn't an appropriate and healthful use of medication, let's remember that we're trying to hold all of this without judgment and with curiosity. Just for the moment, we are going to focus on noticing that this is a thing that people do. (And for what it's worth, the more you work with this image, the more empathy you'll uncover for people in deep pain who are seeking relief, even in ways that don't make sense to you.)

Let's imagine that the pain that we're experiencing isn't a physical pain, so Tylenol isn't going to touch it. We've been excluded, or we're feeling angry, or someone's let us down. What's in the medicine cabinet for this kind of hurt?

This is the point at which Acceptance Commitment Therapy issues us an interesting invitation to slow down and notice how we're medicating our pain. What is the connection between our inner experience and our outer actions? If I'm feeling sad or lonely or angry or resentful, what am I going to do to try to relieve myself of this feeling?

When we accept this invitation and slow down, we might notice some surprising items showing up in our cabinet. We might be treating our loneliness with social media, or our sadness with sleep. Our anger might show up in our language or physical actions, like banging doors or loudly and pointedly unloading a dishwasher. This is where drug and alcohol use can show up, or rage cleaning, or online shopping—they can all be responses to unbearable pain.

If we can notice this connection between our inner and outer experience, between what we feel and what we do, it opens up some other interesting questions. We might notice that these medications come with some side effects. If I'm angry, and I seek relief from my anger through yelling, I might feel shame. Shame might make me want to isolate myself, which will make me feel lonely. How am I then going to medicate this loneliness? I might drink and stay out too late, and then struggle at work the next day and feel bad about that. And so it goes.

It's a very human thing to do; we often find ourselves ping-ponging back and forth between having a feeling and medicating it and then having another related feeling and medicating that. Sometimes it feels like we spend most of our lives in this ping-pong state, medicating the side effects of our last medication.

It's exhausting, isn't it? Let's hit a metaphorical pause button, giving ourselves a moment to catch our breath, clear our systems of the medications, and get off this emotional hamster wheel. It gives us a chance to ask, with curiosity and no judgment, a really important question: "How is this working for me?"

For simplicity's sake, let's say that there are three possible answers here. Let's start in the middle with a neutral response. It's not necessarily working for us, but it's not actively harming us either. Let's say that we're feeling bad about ourselves after making mistakes at work. We come home and medicate our discomfort with takeout and a movie. We get a moment of respite from our discomfort, we don't feel particularly terrible about it, but we have the next day at work looming in front of us and our feelings about that haven't changed. So nothing's shifted, but no harm has been done. I think most of us could live with that; certainly, there's room for this kind of neutral moment in real life. Not every moment can be revelatory.

How do we slip out of neutral and into negative? How do we know when something really isn't working for us? We might notice that we are numbed or distracted for a moment, but pretty soon the side effects kick in, and a different kind of suffering shows up. If we go back to the above example, let's say that we stay up all night binge-watching a new show. It does the trick for us in the moment—it distracts us from our uncomfortable feelings. But then we feel terrible (and show up terribly at work the next day). Or perhaps we snap at our partner who is trying to support us, or we get drunk because we can't bear sitting with our feelings of anxiety and unworthiness.

We might feel our choices are mostly neutral, but they add up in terms of opportunity costs, meaning that we realize we're spending most of our time on things that don't feel meaningful and are mostly about medicating our state. None of these choices make us evil, and all of them are things that humans do to try to get rid of painful experiences. It's also true that none of them serve to shift our pain or move us forward.

The third possible answer is that we do something that actually does relieve us of some pain or at least helps us cope with the pain differently. We somehow find that magic medicine that doesn't really have side effects and doesn't turn us into hamsters trying to outrun emotions on our wheel. This sounds unlikely, but the good news is there is definitely medicine out there that will work for us. The less good (or less convenient) news is that taking it generally requires effort.

What I mean by this is that the actions we take that will help us with our pain and keep us moving toward meaning are usually deeply connected to our values, to who and what is important to us. In the world of Acceptance Commitment Therapy, we might call these values moves or bold moves. These are promises that we make and keep to ourselves, actions that are connected to who we want to be.

What does this look like in real life? Let's say I'm the person who made a mistake at work, and I'm feeling terrible about it. At home I'm distracted and withdrawn, and then I feel guilty because I'm not showing up for my family. At some point I'm able to take a breath, hit the pause button, and notice what's happening. I can then ask myself what values moves are available to me. Is there an accountability piece waiting for me—an apology I can make or a mistake I can put right? Can I acknowledge to my family what's been going on and prioritize connection with them? Perhaps my system does need a bit of a reset, so instead of watching TV all night I watch one episode. These values moves might not eradicate my painful experience, but they might help me feel more like me and the person I want to be.

Sometimes it's helpful to give ourselves a bit of a buffer when trying to figure out what values move we want to try. If I've iden-tified that being creative is important to me, but I'm feeling stuck about what to do about it, I might get bogged down in past mistakes or negative self-talk. So, I can ask myself *What would a person who's creative do?* If I want to be more connected with my family, I could ask *If I watched someone who was very connected in the way I'd like to be, what would I see them doing?* I can try out some of these things with an experimental spirit to see if they work for me or not. The key thing is to try—and to hold outcomes lightly and with curiosity.

With practice and awareness, eventually I'll be able to spend less time on the hamster wheel, and I'll notice early on when I'm taking a medication that's not going to work for me. Hopefully, with even more practice and awareness, I'll be able to notice before I take it, but it's okay if I don't start there.

We can also play with the idea of a dose of medication. If there's something we know that we need but we have a hard time getting, that can bring up a lot of big feelings that can start us running on the hamster wheel. Can we identify what kind of dose is required to meet our need? Can we be creative and flexible about how we get that dose?

Let's use an example of someone who experiences a lot of anxi-ety in relationship and who feels the need for constant communi-cation to medicate that anxiety. Unfortunately, their partner can't meet the need and so they feel lonely and dissatisfied most of the time. They might be stuck in a pattern where they feel bad about themselves for having that need, and the people close to them feel frustrated because nothing they do seems to meet the need. This type of dynamic leads to so much conflict in relationships and to the kinds of conversations that start off with "You never" or "You always." We might throw in some criticism of the person's character ("You're so selfish") or maturity ("You're behaving like a baby").

Let's imagine what it might look like if we took a dose approach to this conversation. First, if I'm the one struggling with the unmet need, I have to respect the fact that this need is there. I can't magic it away or pretend I don't have it. So, I identify it. I name it as my need, and I don't have to justify it or connect it to anyone else's behaviour right now. I can share this with my partner and either make some suggestions about how they can support me with this need or ask what they think might be workable.

It might sound like, "It's really hard for me when you're travelling for work. I think it would help if you sent more texts while you're away. What do you think?"

That gives my partner room to say, "I could give you a good morning and a good night text. Would that help? During the day I'm going to be focused on work, and I don't want to disappoint you or leave you hanging."

This may not be exactly what I imagined or longed for, but it's a good place to start, and it's an experiment worth trying.

Let's flip the script for a moment. Let's say it's my partner who's having a hard time. I may not understand why. I don't need to understand why in order to respect the need and offer responses to it.

If my partner said, "I just found out I'm allergic to shellfish, so please don't put shrimp in the stir-fry," I wouldn't argue about it. I wouldn't accuse them of being weak or not trying hard enough. I would meet that need.

We can respond to emotional needs in much the same way. If we approach our partner's requests with respect and open-mindedness, we can often figure out a solution that's workable for us and respects our capacity and boundaries, and also gives our partner the dose of connection or whatever else they need.

We can use this idea of doses in lots of other ways, of course. We might be able to identify the most workable dose of exercise that helps us start our day off in a good frame of mind or the optimal dose of socializing that leaves us feeling connected and not wiped out. We might notice that a small dose of news mid-morning helps us feel engaged and informed, while a huge dose of news (like what happens when we get glued to our screens for hours at a time) leaves us feeling raw, angry, and dysregulated. The key is to approach needs or emotions, whether they're ours or other people's, with compassion, curiosity, and respect.

Try this

If you're looking for a shortcut version of this process, think of the Three Cs:

Centre

Clarify

Choose

When we notice that we're caught up in a big feeling and that we're moving toward medicating it, the first thing we can do is centre ourselves. That means taking a deep breath, connecting with our senses, and bringing ourselves into the present moment. Next, we clarify what values are at play in that moment. What feels important right now? What are our choices, and which ones feel like values moves? Finally, we choose. We look at the values moves available to us, figure out the workable dose for that moment, and then choose to put it into action.

Imagine a video game

I must confess that the last video game I really got into was *Asteroids* (and I'd like you to know that I was incredibly good at it). Some people close to me are avid gamers, and they recently showed me just how far video games have come. Playing a game of theirs, I felt like I was a character in a movie; the landscapes that I moved through were so detailed and realistic. I got a chance to inhabit a role, and I was surprised at how high stakes the quests felt. If I talked to the right person I would get the keys to the kingdom. If I talked to the wrong person? Dead.

There was something about the intensity of the game-playing experience, the tension I felt when I had to make choices for my character, that made me think about the decision-making landscapes I navigate in everyday life. The choices we encounter day to day don't usually involve a threat of sudden death, but from within the moment of choice they can feel all-important. In our lifetime we may have a handful of truly significant decisions to make, but our modern world encourages us to bring that same intensity to a hundred small decisions every day. Within the context of a game, this might be fun. Within the context of our lives, it's exhausting, it's impossible, it's a giant waste of our time and energy, and it's unworkable.

We wonder if taking that promotion will destroy our relationship or if sending a child to the local kindergarten will doom their job prospects twenty years down the line. If we eat the wrong food we might die prematurely, and if we use the wrong food containers we might expose our family to something toxic. Our lives are packed to the brim with choices that appear to be vital, and we may find ourselves treating every choice as somehow connected to our values, to our identities, or to some sense of morality.

What might be more true is that many of our choices are not really between open strongboxes or death and aren't connected in any meaningful way to our identity or our value system. The world around us may want to frame it all in this way, so that we keep striving and working and buying and moving, but the likelihood is that (if we're looking at daily decision-making) whatever is behind Door #1 is probably not all that different from what's behind Door #2. The outcomes associated with the various choices are pretty much the same, especially if we look a week, a month, or a year ahead.

How do we recognize this in the moment? How can we keep ourselves from bringing video game intensity to Door #1 choices? Perhaps we can use the idea of a volume dial to bring down the intensity we're feeling. We can notice when we're using language that's associated with good/bad frameworks and try swapping out that language for words that are more associated with workability. Workability is a useful lens to look through, and it automatically includes our own experience as something of value that's worth considering.

Let me give you an example of what I'm talking about. Let's say we're working with a young person who is agonizing about which job to take for the summer. The first job probably will sound a bit better on a résumé and is an hour's commute away. The second is a job they've done before and liked and is in their neighbourhood. They're inclined to go back to the work they've done before, but family and friends are pushing them to be more ambitious.

We could apply all sorts of different lenses to this and come up with wildly different thoughts. If we're thinking "Growth Mindset," we might push for the new opportunity. And that wouldn't necessarily be wrong! If we focus on workability, however, what shows up?

In this case, this person thought, *I have one more summer before I go away, and I don't want to be spending two hours a day commuting. What's most workable right now is a job that is easy to get to, so I can make the money I need for school AND see my friends.* They were able to let go of the other possibility with just a whiff of regret and ended up having a fantastic summer.

It's kind of fun to imagine this kind of scenario as part of a true-to-life video game. Push yourself to your max and be very stressed while doing so—and watch your emotion points dwindle to nothing.

Or ask yourself what's workable and treat your own time and energy as worthy of respect—and win everything you need to keep on playing.

Let's keep playing with this image, only this time let's focus on gaming our way through discomfort. I know that sounds much less appealing, and yet it opens up so much freedom to us, once we let go of the idea that there's one particular path that's free of any discomfort, stress, or pain.

Often when we're making choices, we're picking something that presents itself as more comfortable, that avoids the sticky moment or the painful conversation. We think, *I'll just go along with this now because I don't want to seem rude*, and then we end up in a moment that we never would have chosen for ourselves. It's sort of like getting stuck at that same place in our video game for weeks and weeks because we don't think we have the skills to level up. We get so frustrated, and the fun drains right out of the experience.

We might try to ignore someone's behaviour that's actually really hurtful because we think we can make it fine and it would feel strange to say something. Then weeks later, after a steady stream of small unkindnesses, we hit our wall and blow up.

I'm sure you've experienced many situations where you put off the uncomfortable moment, pushing it off into the shadows where it grew until it came back into your life, ten times as large and a hundred times more painful.

So, let's imagine, the next time we run into this type of choice, trying to do something that's a little different. The first thing we might need to do is slow down and notice that we're moving toward avoidance. We can generally tell if we pay attention to the language we're using. If we catch ourselves saying or thinking something like, *No, no—I'm fine* or *I don't want this to be awkward* or *I shouldn't be upset about this*, the next question we could ask is *What am I trying to avoid right now?* (I can add that at this point I have an almost Pavlovian response to the words "fine" and "should," which works well for me but probably gets annoying for people around me. Some friends and I now say "fine-fine" to indicate when we're actually okay, and "fine-not-fine" when something bad has happened, we are coping, and we want to process it, but don't have time to at that moment.)

In any case, once we've named it, there's no rush to take action. It might make sense to get a little curious first, to understand more about why we might want to avoid it. Are we afraid? Do we have some lived experience with this type of thing, with this kind of process? Have we played this type of game before? What happened when we did?

Let's explore a scenario to understand how all of this might play out in real life. You have a dear friend whom you often meet up with, and she's always late. Sometimes it's just a few minutes but sometimes it's thirty minutes or even an hour. She seems so nonchalant about it, so you don't say anything in the moment when it happens. But on the inside, you're irritated, and it's showing up in how you're connecting with her. There's a story building up in your brain, a story about her selfishness, laziness, and lack of consideration, and that story translates into how you speak to her.

You often do end up having fun after the bumpy start because she's entertaining and energetic and you have a deep history together. Your feelings about that internal story are building, however, and you start saying no to invitations from her. Gradually your relationship starts fading away, without the two of you ever talking about it. You miss her vibrancy and all that the relationship brought to your life, and when you think of her there's a sadness.

Let's imagine taking that sadness, that moment of discomfort and pain, and picking it up and moving it way earlier in the timeline. Maybe we move it to a moment early on when the two of you were meeting up and she was thirty minutes late. It feels uncomfortable to say something, but you take a deep breath and try. You want to come at it from a curious, open stance. It might sound something like, "I'm noticing you're showing up later and later when we're meeting. Have you noticed? I'd like to know what you think about this."

All you're doing is naming something you've noticed, and asking what she's seeing. You haven't yet said anything about any impact on you, though you absolutely could. This is where the "I statements" beloved by so many therapists could show up, where you name what you're feeling without making assumptions about her actions or feelings. You're leaving the door wide open for her to come in and say what's going on for her.

It might be that she's dealing with unpredictable travel times or that she honestly had no idea this was going on. She may have grown up in a family where lateness was not a big issue. She may have ideas about contexts where it's okay to be late (like meeting you at your house) and where it's not (meeting you on a street corner). She might share something that helps you change your internal story about it and also helps the two of you work out something together that suits you both.

It might also be true that she hears your question and gets angry, feels judged, and pulls away. Hopefully, there will be room to explore this (and we'll talk about images and metaphors later to assist with these sorts of explorations), but here's the thing: if a relationship ends because you've tried to have a compassionate, curious conversation about boundary setting, it was going to end at some point anyway.

Let's come back to our metaphor. On our screen we see a prompt that gives us a choice. "Say to your friend you're wondering why she's often late" or "Say nothing to your friend, sit and seethe in silence, and then refuse the next invitation." You can substitute a similar situation from your own life. What's the title of your game? What are your options? How do you think each of these stories will end?

An image I sometimes layer on top of this exploration is that of a controlled avalanche. A client once described their experience of anger as an avalanche descending, which was such a great image to bring in, and it inspired us to keep going with that exploration.

Neither of us in that session knew much about real avalanches, so we gave ourselves permission to make some stuff up. We imagined that if actual experts were to see evidence that an avalanche was going to happen, they would take action to prevent the worst harm from occurring. They might do a risk assessment, they'd use all their prior knowledge to set things up properly, they would do what they needed to do to protect people, and then they would take action to allow the avalanche to happen in the least harmful way possible. What we sincerely hoped they would not do is see the danger but refuse to do anything because it might be awkward or uncomfortable. (And of course as soon as I say this, many events come to mind when people who should know better DID turn a blind eye to what needed to be done because they were trying to avoid certain responses or consequences; those moments don't disprove the metaphor, but they do provoke an irritation that feels more like a distraction in this moment, so I'll hit the pause button on them for now.)

How do we know when there's an avalanche looming in our own life and it might be time to take action? Our bodies will tell us, if we're open to listening to what they're saying. We might feel tightness in our jaw, a sickness in our stomach, or a dull buzzing in our brain. Cues might show up in our behaviour; we might be slamming the dishwasher shut, have trouble falling asleep at night, or wrenching cupboard doors open. We might be curt with our language, or we might find ourselves on the verge of tears for what feels like no reason in a particular moment.

Once we notice these cues, and treat them with the curiosity and respect they deserve, what happens next? We know our emotions need to move, just like the snow does, and we also know we are seeking to limit harm. We might spend some time on our own trying to name and know what's at the heart of what we're feeling. We may need help with that, and so we can turn to a therapist or a friend or a trusted advisor. We most likely need to take time and space to tend to our system, so that we feel as regulated and connected as possible. So, we invite in some delight—we listen to music, we taste wonderful things, we tend to our bodies, we smell something delicious—and when we feel just that little bit more in tune with ourselves, we can step toward the necessary conversation. That conversation could start, just as in the example shared earlier, with a simple statement related to what we've been noticing and feeling, and a question about what's happening for the other person. Ideally, this conversation happens when both participants have time and space for it, and there is room for anyone involved to come and go as per their needs, as long as that is communicated with care.

Our hope for this conversation is not to avoid any discomfort; rather, it's to set the conversation up so that the discomfort can be tolerated. One of the very best things I learned in therapy school was about how this process actually strengthens a relationship. All true relationships must experience cycles of rupture and repair. If they don't, then someone in the relationship doesn't feel safe enough to be honest, and so there are limits on how deep and true that relationship can be. Now, not all relationships need to be deep and true.

If you have a boss you don't really trust but you need your job, honour your instincts and let the relationship be what it is.

Perhaps you can think of it this way: each time you engage in a rupture and repair cycle with someone dear to you, the safety net underneath your relationship gets stronger and stronger. A strong safety net just might make it easier for you and your person to have even more fun together and enjoy even better connections.

If you love someone and are trying to build strong connections with them, at some point you'll have a choice between erasing yourself or stepping toward a rupture and repair conversation. I think you know which one will get you further in this game.

Try this

Is there an uncomfortable conversation you've been avoiding in your own life? Is there something painful that's happening with someone close to you? What might it look like to talk about it with that person? What could help it feel like productive, not toxic discomfort? What feels risky about it? What might be the reward?

Imagine a beautiful place

Let's begin by imagining a beautiful place. When we're there we feel calm, safe, joyful, and relaxed. It could be a made-up place, it could resemble a place we've been to but not be exactly the same, or it could be a place we know well. If it is a place we know well, let's choose a place that's fairly uncomplicated. Sometimes people choose an old family cottage, for example, and then memories of old arguments with relatives intrude on the process. Or we imagine a place we loved that's not available to us anymore, and sadness shows up. Let's allow ourselves a moment of true respite, and choose a place where we genuinely feel at ease.

Some people gravitate to the ocean or to a lake. Others find themselves in a forest. Some locate themselves in a beautiful library, a place with spiritual meaning, or a corner of their own home. I find myself imagining a screened-in porch, similar to but not exactly like ones I've known in the past.

This image, like the container visualization we explored before, is also drawn from the world of EMDR, although the idea of visualizing a calm or beautiful place is found in many meditative or contemplative traditions. As with the container image, when we are in the resourcing phase of EMDR, we will often work on developing a mental model of a calm place or a beautiful place—an image that we can invoke to help us take care of our system in a moment of need. I find this very useful in places like a doctor's office, or if I'm stuck on public transit somewhere, or waiting for an important phone call or meeting. What I love about this process is the way we layer on sensory components one by one; it makes for a very rich and satisfying experience.

Once we've chosen our place, we let our mind's eye take a look around, and we name what we see. If you're at the ocean, you may see colourful beach umbrellas, bright fish in the water nearby, or palm trees swaying in the breeze. In a library you may see people quietly reading at great wooden tables, and shelves and shelves of books covering the walls. When I look around me on my screened-in porch, I see a comfortable chair with a small table beside it, with books and a nice mug of coffee waiting for me. Through the screen I see green trees and blue sky, and cheeky squirrels grabbing their lunches from the ground before darting back to safety in the trees.

We take our time appreciating what we can see, and then we might turn our attention to what we can hear. Do we hear the wind or the songs of birds? Do we hear happy murmurs from other people, far enough away to be pleasant and not intrusive? We may notice the sound of water moving or of someone in the kitchen making us a delicious lunch. There could be light rain hitting the roof over our heads. Can we take a breath and really listen?

Next, we can imagine what something in this place feels like. What does it feel like to reach down and scoop some sand up from the beach, and let it trickle through our fingers? If we trail our hands through the water, is it cool? If there is a railing on a deck that we're standing on, can we feel what it's like to hold it firmly? What do we notice under our hands? What does the wind feel like ruffling our hair?

Now we can take a big deep breath in, and perhaps we smell something. It could be freshly made coffee, it could be the salty tang of the sea, or it could be a perfectly ripe mango waiting for us to try it. We might smell that particular aroma that shows up in spring when the snow is melting and things are starting to grow again. We might notice the scent of a candle, a favourite food, or a beautiful flower. Take a breath and then another. What do you notice?

And now we might run our tongue around the inside of our mouth. Do we taste that coffee that was waiting for us in the mug on the side table? Or is it the flavour of that perfect mango? What taste would we welcome? What taste might feel like comfort or care?

We may want to give our beautiful place a name, so that we can invoke it or invite it in quickly when we need to go there. When I think of "screened-in porch" I immediately feel a response in my system. Yours may be "by the beach" or "hotel room" or "mountain top." Whatever it is, once you've named it, keep visiting it whenever you have a bit of space. With time, attention, and practice, you'll have created a wonderful resource for yourself that you can go to whenever you need.

Try this

Where is your beautiful place?

What do you see when you look around?

What do you hear?

When you reach out your hands, what can you touch?

When you take a deep breath in, what do you smell?

When you run your tongue around your mouth, what can you taste?

What name will you give your beautiful place?

Imagine a tape recorder

I'm imagining an old-fashioned tape recorder right now, with huge clunky buttons that make a satisfying sound when you push them down. What I want us to focus on first is the pause button.

Have you ever had the experience of being in a conflict with someone and watching things escalate, feeling somewhat helpless to stop what's happening? We notice a horrible, painful, fiery feeling inside, and maybe we aren't feeling seen or heard or understood, and we want to get rid of that fire, so we throw it at the other person. But it doesn't get rid of our pain or our fire. It sets the other person ablaze instead.

Imagine we're listening to a recording of this conflict. One person is on fire, and you hear them gearing up, ready to spread the fire, rage in their voice. This is where we imagine that big old pause button. We notice the pain, we notice the fire, and then instead of accepting the next moment as inevitable, we hit pause. CLICK.

We take a breath. The pain is legitimate. We are not ignoring it or erasing it. We are pausing.

We tell the other person what we're doing. We might say, "This is going too far too fast. I don't like how this is rolling out. I'm going to hit pause." Hitting pause might mean sitting in silence for a moment and taking a deep breath. It might mean one or both people taking a few minutes for a short walk or a drink of water. We can imagine the fire dying down with nothing showing up to feed it.

If you're in conflict with someone close to you, this idea of the pause button ideally is something you've incorporated into your shared vocabulary, so the other person knows what is happening and doesn't feel abandoned or ignored. Earlier, when we explored the idea of creating a container for our thoughts, we discussed the value of practicing skills outside of challenging moments. Working with a pause button is an excellent example of a skill that benefits from practice, especially in close relationships. Getting both people used to the idea that conversations can be paused and resumed, and giving both people the chance to experience what happens when we come back to difficult conversations with more clarity and groundedness (i.e., less destructive conflict) makes it more likely that we'll be able to use this skill when we're activated.

What might practice look like? It might sound like, "This is an important conversation, and I really want to be paying attention, but I'm distracted by having to leave for work. Can I hit pause on it, and we can talk about it after lunch?"

Or it could sound like, "I can tell you're upset, and I would love to talk this through with you. I'd like to hit pause until we're in the same room, and I can see what's going on with you more clearly."

To be clear, we always have the right to hit pause in a conversation, whether it's something we've discussed and practiced with the other person previously or not. If a conversation is going off the rails, hit pause! You don't need permission.

If you're dealing with someone close to you, though, it's worth investing time to develop this skill together and practicing so that you both know what it feels like not just to pause a conversation but to resume it. The first time you try pausing a big conversation, the other person can experience some really complicated and painful feelings. If they grew up with unpredictable or absent caregivers, they might feel abandoned or isolated. Being transparent about your intentions here, being specific about how much time you'll be taking and when you'll come back, and then following through on what you promised might help them tolerate the pause more easily. Once they see that the conversation was paused—not erased or silenced—and that the resumed conversation worked better, their trust in the process can grow.

One client asked me, "What's the difference between this and what I grew up with—the abrupt change of subject when something got uncomfortable? I hated that!"

It's a good question, and I do think there's an important difference here worth exploring. The passive-aggressive "Oh, let's talk about something nice!" is an erasure. It's pretending that everything is okay when it's not. The person who's in pain sees the opportunity to be seen and understood and cared for slipping out of reach. The fire gets covered up, but it continues to burn.

When we say we are hitting pause, the implicit promise is that it's a pause, not a stop. We are saying we will come back to it when we have capacity. For this to work, we have to keep the promise. We have to make full use of the time and the grace the pause gives us to regulate and to take care of ourselves, so that we can come back and hit the play button.

Next, let's think about the volume dial. I talk about volume dials with people when they're having a hard time loving a part of themselves. For example, someone might be coming to therapy because they hate their anxiety and want to get rid of it. So, we'll take some time to understand the impact anxiety is having on them and to notice and appreciate the related losses they've experienced. Through these conversations, they might start noticing that their anxiety feels like a problem when the volume dial on it is turned up super high. At other moments, when the volume's low, their anxiety might show up in a way that feels and looks different. It might show up as consideration, sensitivity, or efficiency. It might show up as parts of them that they actually like.

So the conversation shifts; we leave behind the idea that there's a part of ourselves that's so unlovable that we have to get rid of it, and we start thinking about how we can work respectfully and lovingly with our volume dials, so that when something starts feeling too loud or too much, we know how to work with our own systems to turn it down.

Part of why I think this is effective is because it takes away moral judgments or negative self-talk that we might be engaging in when we're caught up in a big feeling, whether it's anxiety, anger, sadness, fear, or any other emotion that feels overwhelming. We don't have to be disappointed with ourselves that we couldn't keep our feelings at bay. That's not something that is possible for humans to do. Perhaps instead we can meet our emotions with curiosity, and even in that moment when the dial is turned way up, ask ourselves why this feeling is surfacing right here right now.

What might we do to turn down the volume a little? Cold temperatures can be helpful; we could run our hands under cold water or rest our wrists on an ice pack. We can move our tongue around our mouths a little, which makes our body generate saliva, which, in turn, is a cue for our body to start thinking about resting, digesting, and getting calmer. We could go for a walk, or if that's not available, we could find a gentle way of moving our bodies. We could squeeze and release our hands, for example, or rise up on our toes and then let our bodies fall back down so that our heels land solidly on the ground. We can give ourselves a few moments to focus on our breathing.

How else might this image of the volume dial help us? Let's be quite literal for a moment; the experience we're having might be causing us to yell or be loud ourselves, and we may not be getting the response we were hoping for or that we need. I think it's interesting to experiment sometimes with the volume and tone of our voices and see how easily we can alter the meaning of what we're saying without changing the words at all.

For example, imagine someone yelling at you, "Why do you never have your work done on time?" The volume dial is WAY up, and their tone is furious. The conversation has just started, and it's already a fight. Your system is elevated, and it certainly sounds like theirs is too. You might have a good reason for missing your deadline, but do you feel safe sharing that now?

Now imagine the same person saying the same thing, but in a quiet, friendly tone. The word "never" might rub you the wrong way a little, but let's say you can really hear the concern in their voice. Now it might feel a bit different, and you might feel like there's room for you to say what you're struggling with.

This happens with clients a lot; they'll be yelling things like, "What kind of person makes this kind of mistake?" They are so, so loud and angry with themselves. I might say that this is a really good question, and then I might ask them to consider what would it feel like to ask themselves that same question in a gentle, supportive tone of voice? When we turn the volume down in this way, we make room for genuine emotion and genuine understanding. The answer to the first loud angry question might be "A STUPID person!" which is pretty hard to work with. The answer to the second gentle question could be something like, "A human being who was trying but needed more time," and that answer gives us somewhere to go.

Can you imagine this sort of question, a question you might have for yourself? It might start out with, "What kind of person _____?"

Here's a personal example for you. I might ask, "What kind of person says she'd like to write a book and then doesn't DO anything about it for two years!?" I can shout it at myself, saying it in a very critical and hurtful way. Then I can turn the volume down and ask it again, in a kind tone. The answer comes to me then. "A person who was afraid." Ahhh. Okay. That answer gives me somewhere to go.

Try this

Think of something you've said to yourself or to someone else that came out in a loud and angry way. Experiment with saying it in a different tone of voice, at a lower volume, and maybe tweaking the words a little bit. Is there a good question in there that was obscured by your delivery? What does it feel like to ask that question without that protective layer of anger?

Imagine a baby

Imagine the sweet face of a baby. The curve of the cheeks, the bright eyes figuring out the world. Maybe there's some downy hair, or maybe there is a little fist finding its way into a determined mouth.

I would be very surprised and deeply saddened if you were to look at a baby, even if you're not particularly fond of babies, and say something like, "That baby's not very symmetrical." "That baby isn't wearing a very flattering outfit." "Wow, that baby has a weird nose."

Or maybe something a little meaner. "Why does that baby think they can get away with wearing that?" "That baby's profile is so ugly." "Look at that baby showing off." "Why does that baby think they're so important?"

These just aren't things we generally say about babies. And yet, these are things I hear people say about other people or about themselves all the time.

I do too, sometimes. I say some pretty terrible things about my-self every once in a while. When I see my own baby photos, I don't think hateful or critical things. I was pretty cute! I bet you were too. And yet when I look at my adult self, a physical self that came into being without me really doing anything to create or shape it, some very unkind things float into my mind.

At what point did I decide it was okay to say these things to myself? At what point do any of us decide that it's okay to level our judgment against someone's physical self, whether it's a stranger on the street or our own self in the mirror?

If we were to look at one of those sped-up photo montages that races through a person's life, one photo per month from birth to adulthood, would there be a moment when we would hit pause and say, "Now, THIS is the exact moment when this person became eligible for my contempt and criticism"? I think it would be pretty hard to pinpoint that moment and pretty revealing if we noticed an age or a stage when suddenly criticism felt appropriate instead of warped.

Let's agree, even for a moment, that such a moment doesn't need to come. We don't ever need to hit pause and make room for judgment and contempt. If we look at a baby with awe and wonder, with delight and appreciation and love, we can look at each other and at ourselves in the same way.

It can be very illuminating and emotional to look at an image of yourself as a baby, and then try to bring that same gaze to your face in the mirror. This can be a painful exercise for many people, especially if you weren't cherished in childhood the way you should have been. You may be able to trace the origin of those critical thoughts, those hateful judgments, right back to someone who should have been able to look at you with unconditional love. Please know that the words you hear and carry now that cloud your ability to see your true self clearly were never about you. They were always a reflection of someone else's pain and discontent with their own selves.

It feels so bitterly ironic that other people's inability to love themselves may be what blocks us from loving ourselves. Our culture makes it hard to even talk about this. Any concept or act related to love or care for the self swiftly becomes commodified or ridiculed or diminished in some way. We feel absurd and vulnerable and foolish when we start trying to treat ourselves with love instead of disdain, when we try to keep the promises we make to ourselves or speak to ourselves in a loving way. We might not even know ourselves well enough to know what we like or want.

Maybe we can start by asking ourselves the question, "If I really loved myself, how would that show up in what I do?" Or if that seems too painful, we could try, "What would someone who loved themselves do? What does it feel like when I do the same things?" Maybe if we allow ourselves the experience of behaving as if we loved ourselves, we might almost accidentally back into the actual feeling one day. It's sort of like when we're learning to take care of a baby. We might not know anything when we start, but we learn to run through a mental checklist when babies show us that they need something. Are they hungry, are they tired, are they wet, are they too hot, are they too cold, do they have gas, are they uncomfortable, or do they want to be cuddled? We try all the things, and hopefully something clicks and the baby is happier. Would this work for ourselves? Do we even know what's on our own checklist?

As I write this, it occurs to me that we often use the words "Don't be a baby" as a kind of insult or criticism. It's interesting to think about why these words are wielded like this and what happens if we spend some time with this idea. What is so terrible about being like a baby? What is so terrible about sleeping when we're tired, eating when we're hungry, wearing comfortable clothes all the time, showing our emotions when we feel them, and enjoying lots of cuddles with people we love? When we say "Don't be a baby," perhaps what we are saying is "Want less. Need less. Ask for less." If we're saying it to someone else, it might be that their needs feel inconvenient to us. Maybe we could talk about not being able to meet these needs rather than criticizing the needs themselves. If we're saying it to ourselves, what unmet need are we trying to erase? When we are asked how we are, how many times have we answered, "I'm fine!" when the truth is that we're not fine at all?

All of this also makes me think of a pattern I often see in my work with families; parents will become very focused and anxious on a milestone they're hoping their baby will achieve. If the baby achieves it, there is a short, sweet moment of celebrating, and then the focus shifts to the next milestone to worry about. Parents don't really give themselves much time to rejoice and savour any particular milestone or moment. And yet, the fact that someone learned how to roll, to smile, or to jump is still amazing! If I ever jump for any reason (usually a kitchen dance party) I often think of what an incredible moment it is when someone realizes that they can separate themselves from gravity temporarily. Who was the first to figure that out? How is it possible that humans and animals keep figuring this out? How fantastic is that?

This reveals something that so many of us do, something that is profoundly human but also serves to steal joy away from us. We long for something, we work for it, and as soon as we achieve it we look for the next thing. We forget almost instantaneously the depth of our previous longing, the work we did to move forward, and the flash of joy we experienced when we arrived at our goal. Are we afraid of staying for a moment in joy? What might it look like if we allow ourselves to linger even one minute longer in a place of appreciation and delight? What might it feel like if we looked at ourselves and saw a beautiful, priceless collection of lessons learned and achievements unlocked, instead of moving instantly to the next item on our "to achieve" list?

No part of this discussion is meant to make us feel guilty or bad about having these normal human responses, experiencing certain thought patterns, or noticing critical self-talk. It's okay if those words show up, whether we're talking ourselves out of needing something or we notice hateful self-criticism floating into our awareness. It's painful, but it's human. As we've discussed before, we don't have all that much control over what words, ideas, or thoughts float in. Many of these ways of speaking and thinking about needs and goals and physical selves are so embedded in our culture that it feels impossible to escape them entirely.

Let's recognize these words as useless babble, as irritating ads that interrupt what we really want to hear. When these annoying ads come on, try turning that volume dial down to zero. Don't let these ads, these manipulative lies, steal your sense of who you truly are. Stand in front of a mirror. Let yourself be with your own face and frame for a moment. See what it feels like to connect with your own bright eyes, still figuring out the world.

Try this

Do you have a baby picture of yourself? What does it feel like to look at it? Look at your eyes in your picture and then at your eyes in a mirror. What do you see? What do you feel?

Imagine a baseball

The first draft of this book was (as many first drafts are) very different from what you're reading now, and it had a different title. I had called it *Hold It Lightly*, which is one of my very favourite phrases. These words cross my mind many times a day—when I'm listening to feedback, taking in news, or responding to something that I find irritating or triggering. Wiser heads convinced me that this phrase wasn't going to work as a title for this book, but I still wanted to share it with you.

What does it feel like to hold something lightly, and why do I want to explore this practice with you? When I share this thought, this invitation to hold something lightly, some people respond to it right away like they're thirsty and it's water. Others respond with almost a kind of revulsion. They have a feeling that they're being told that something about themselves or what's happened to them is not important. Let's step toward that, gently and with curiosity.

Imagine something coming at you. It could be words, criticism, feedback, a diagnosis, advice, reviews, or instructions. It could be rejection, cruelty, stupidity, wisdom, kindness. It could be an emotion or a response. It could be love, hate, need, or want. It could be coming from someone else, or it could be coming from you to you. Whatever it is, imagine it as an object. Let's pick something to make it easier to visualize. Imagine a baseball landing in your hands.

This baseball could have been tossed gently, or it could have been hurled at you with enormous force or speed, which may be what you're used to. If that's the case, you might feel inclined to throw it right back with equal force. But let's give ourselves a moment here.

In this moment, let's imagine everything slowing down, so that this particular moment becomes infinitely large. Inside the largeness of this moment, you may find space and flexibility. You may find some choices appearing.

The way this baseball ended up in your hands doesn't dictate what you have to do with it next. You can hang onto it or drop it. You don't need to let it get close; you don't need to allow it near your actual self. You can hold it lightly, hold it away from your body, or drop it, and you may notice that when you do that, you have an opportunity to observe it, to be curious about it.

If you hold it lightly, if you resist clutching onto it and drawing it in, you're giving yourself a choice. You don't have to allow someone else's need to give to force you to take.

There is a difference between holding something lightly and holding something carelessly. There is a world of care in how you hold lightly anything you're imagining—it's just that some of that care is directed toward yourself.

Some of the questions you can ask yourself are: Is this something actually meant for me? If I keep it, will it be helpful for me? Could it harm me? Can I learn from it? Is it something I can throw to another person? What do I think the other person wants me to do with it? What do I want to do with it? Often, when someone throws us a baseball, we automatically move to throw it back because of course that's what you do with a baseball. But we're not in the ninth inning of a World Series game here, so there's no rush. We can take time to be curious.

Maybe this baseball isn't for us, and the next thing for us to do is figure out who to throw it to or if it's okay for us to let it drop on the floor and roll away. This often came up when I was working in the hospital and talking with people who were angry or upset. They would come in and just whip that verbal fastball right at me. If I was able to catch it and hold it, I often found that that was all that needed to be done. They just wanted someone to catch what they were saying. Once they had that experience, they were usually able to take the baseball away with them. Sometimes I would help by figuring out who we could throw the ball to next. Did they need help finding resources, the Patient Relations office, or a particular specialist? It took me a long time to figure out that no situation would require me to hang onto that baseball forever.

I often use these words and this imagery in work with couples when they are finding themselves stuck in a pattern of escalating fiery arguments. If you remember our earlier image of the tape recorder, this is when I might ask them to bring that out. I ask them to hit pause and notice what they are throwing at each other and how they're doing it. Do they want to be hurling fastballs at each other? Do they know why they're doing that? Do they think that engaging in this lightning-fast exchange will get their needs met? Are they displaying care for each other in this moment?

I might ask one partner to imagine their words, the words they want to say to their partner, as the baseball resting in their hands. They're holding something that they want their partner to catch, so that it can be seen and understood. It's something important. How can they throw it to their partner so that it can be caught? Will they wind up and throw that baseball straight at their partner's head? It might work better to slow down and prepare their partner for the throw. This might sound like describing their own thoughts and feelings, using those "I statements" we mentioned before, and avoiding assigning motivation or blame to the other person. (And don't be sneaky with "I statements." There's a world of difference between saying something like "I'm feeling overwhelmed" and "I'm feeling overwhelmed by your stupidity.") Then with attention, focus, and good faith, they can let the baseball leave their hands to pass to their partner.

To the partner, I might suggest catching it gently and then taking a moment to hold it before putting it down in a space between them. Take some time to look at it, to get to know it. This might sound like asking open-ended questions. It will definitely sound like curiosity and not defensiveness. There's no need to be defensive at this point, because you're both just looking at a baseball and wondering about it.

After the first partner feels that what they've shared has been caught, seen, and understood, it might be time for the other partner to engage in a similar process, but it can be really helpful to pause for a moment in between throws. We can be tempted into rushing this process because in relationship we have a powerful need to be seen, and if our partner has had that need met, we really want our turn. But speed doesn't work in our favour here, so let this be slow.

Try this

When couples are stuck in a defensive/reactive model in therapy, I sometimes bring this metaphor to life by asking them to pass an object back and forth. The famed couples therapist Esther Perel sometimes introduces a ball into her sessions; you can only speak when you are holding the ball. It introduces a sense of play into the dynamic, and it also slows down the discourse. In my version I might ask clients to pass a pillow between them. I might ask them to describe the pillow as the thing they're feeling. When the other person takes the pillow, they repeat that description. It's interesting how something like adding a ball or a pillow into the discussion can completely change the mood; something fraught becomes friendly. Are there some hard conversations you need to have that might be helped by the inclusion of a playful object?

Imagine a computer

This one is easy for me to imagine because it happened to me this morning as I typed. Something was going on with my computer, and it was sluggish and sticky. My frustration was building. I went onto the Activity Monitor, and I saw hundreds of processes going on all at the same time. I had no idea what most of them were doing, but suddenly I had an inkling about why things were slow. I saved everything that needed to be saved, I exited everything that could be exited, and I turned off the computer. I went for a walk around the block. I said hi to my neighbour and a friendly dog. I came back, made tea, and turned my computer back on. Thank goodness—it worked again. Relief.

It strikes me that what went on with my computer is similar to something I experience fairly regularly. When I'm feeling sluggish and slow or when I'm finding it hard to switch from task to task, it's usually because I have too many things going on at the same time. A background buzz of worry about things that are happening in the world around me and/or with my family. A ticking to-do list that never seems to get shorter. Different streams of life that are all important and all deserve 100 percent of everything but never get it. A long list of "shoulds" that I never seem to get to (Vitamins! Emails! Stretches! Decluttering!).

Every time I switch streams, it's like opening up another process without closing one. It's like a little bit of my focus or energy stays with the previous task even as I move onto the next. How can I reclaim that focus? How can I close these processes?

In her wonderful TED talk about truths she learned from living and writing, Anne Lamott said, "Almost everything will work again if you unplug it for a few minutes, even you." That's exactly what I did this morning when my computer got slow. I noticed my frustration, I paid attention to the slowness, and instead of fighting with it, I treated it like a cue or a prompt. I shut everything down (including me).

It's not always easy to shut everything down, to be honest. You might be carrying a heavy burden of worry or pain, and to shut down the emotional processes related to that may seem impossible or feel inappropriate or disrespectful. In some moments the work that needs to be done is to be with that pain, to feel it thoroughly. In other moments there may be room for something else.

Two questions I ask myself over and over again to get to that something else are: *Where do I need to be right now?* and *What is this in service of?* The first question is helpful when I'm feeling stuck and am not sure to do next. Focusing on the core work, whether it be grief or joy, heart work or housework, gives me space to bring my attention to the moment and do what needs to be done. I learned it from a parent who had babies in two different hospitals and felt so much guilt at not being able to be with both of them. He grounded himself by asking *Where do I need to be right now?* and then gave himself permission to be where he was, to inhabit that moment fully. It made a hard situation tolerable.

My day-to-day experience is not usually as challenging as that, but it often involves some level of guilt or shame about not doing all the things all the time. When I ask myself that question and give myself that moment, I'm not saying I'll never do those other things that are whispering for attention. I'm just acknowledging that they don't all have to be done right now.

A twist on that question could be *Can I make my peace with where I am right now?* I think this is a beautiful question that can help shut down or pause the energy-wasting, joy-eroding process otherwise known as fear of missing out (FOMO). People hold so much worry and fear around this, that there's always something wonderful going on that they're not invited to, and of course the loud, chaotic 24/7 performative arena of social media serves to turn the volume way up on those awful feelings.

What if I told you that there was no better party, no more important event, than what is available to you in your life right now? That, in fact, the myth of the great party is a constructed one, designed to keep you off-balance and discontented, always seeking something external to your self to alter yourself? What would it look like to make peace with what you are currently experiencing? To find that the joy that you've been told is all the way over there (a place you can't get to) is actually within arm's reach? Think about what appeals to you about the mythic great party and think about how those different pieces might be found closer to home. Connection, appreciation, fun, distraction, meaning—they might be right there in front of you. Let's experiment with treating that feeling, that fear of missing out, as a cue to turn inwards first and be curious about any unmet needs we're experiencing in that moment that we could address in our own environment. We can shut that whole process down, all that energy that we're directing toward an unfulfillable longing, and reclaim the time and space for ourselves.

The second question, *What is this in service of?*, is for when I find myself in the middle of doing something fairly mindless. I might be scrolling on the internet (in fact, nine times out of ten when I ask myself this question I'm doing something like that), or engaging in something without much intention or attention. By asking myself this question, I'm taking a moment to check in with curiosity and little or no judgment. The answer might be *This is helping me relax after a very busy day*, which feels okay, and so I keep going. Sometimes I need some Netflix! The answer might also be *I'm avoiding doing something that matters to me*, which is my invitation to take a deep breath and step toward that task.

If I think about the function of a behaviour (as opposed to assigning any moral qualities to it) it helps me make choices about how I want to spend my time without getting caught up in recriminations and self-loathing. In other words, if I accept that avoiding and distracting are things that ordinary human beings do to themselves all the time, and that I'm not evil but simply human if I do this too, I suddenly have more space to name what's going on and make some choices about what comes next.

Let's keep playing with the idea of a computer or a phone or whatever tech device you prefer. Every time someone tells me, "I'm really broken, and I am hoping you can fix me," my heart breaks a little. I want to show so much respect for that feeling and give so much love to the human who is experiencing it, while at the same time stating with utter honesty and complete conviction that they are not broken. You are not broken. I think I know why you feel that way. It's probably because people around you have said that to you, and your daily lived experience is painful and you hope that it could be different. I really want to honour you, and I want to honour that hope.

If you're not broken, what happens to the idea of fixing? What are we hoping for? If you're not broken, does that mean there's no opportunity for you to make things better for yourself? This is where I think it's interesting to step back to the idea of a computer or a mobile phone.

When we first get a computer or a phone, it might have some core functions on it, and it's shiny and new and does all kinds of neat things. Then we start downloading software and apps onto it. Some of these things are fantastic—they help us read books, listen to music, or connect to people. Some of these things are more complicated. They connect us to people and make us feel terrible about ourselves, or they distract us from big parts of our lives. Sometimes we don't read the agreements thoroughly, so we don't really know what we're downloading, and suddenly we've given away a lot of space without realizing that that's what we were doing. We may also get tricked into downloading viruses or malware—programs that look interesting but are intentionally destructive. Maybe our phone stops working or our computer starts crashing.

When this happens to one of our devices, what can we do? We can get help from someone who knows a lot about technology, and that's an amazing thing to do. They can help us clean stuff up and teach us what to do so that it doesn't happen again. We can also put some effort and intention into uninstalling what we don't want or even go back to the factory settings.

Let's bring this idea back to us. What would it look like for a human to go back to factory settings or to uninstall programs or functions that are causing problems? We might think about our younger selves, about what we loved and what we did before we were taught to criticize ourselves, feel shame, or shrink ourselves. Maybe we look with a neutral and loving gaze at which functions are taking up the most space in our lives and consider whether they are really working for us. Maybe there's a different program we can download that helps us do the same thing but takes up less space?

In other words, maybe there's a different way we can think about this, a kinder value we can invite in, that gives us some more flexibility day to day? Perhaps the most important thing we can do is to name some of our most critical and malevolent inner dialogues as the viruses that they are and by doing so release the hold they have on our sense of self and value. We may or may not be able to trace them back to their origin; sometimes it's really clear where they came from, and sometimes it's a mystery. We don't need to know where they came from to know that they're damaging.

Once we free up some space and we notice our system is up and functioning again, maybe we can make a promise to ourselves to keep paying attention. Maybe we will think twice before trying a new program or app, or we will invest a little time in regular daily or weekly maintenance so that we stop problems before they get big. Let's think about what maintenance means for computers and how we can translate that into our own care.

With a computer, we might think about calendar-based main-tenance, or tasks that are done on a scheduled date to take care of the system. There's predictive maintenance, which thinks ahead to when something might need attention based on past experience. And there's reactive maintenance, which responds to issues after they've emerged. It would be pretty nice to never have to engage with reactive maintenance, but sometimes that's not realistic, espe-cially for human beings.

If I think about how this translates into human activity, I imag-ine scheduling weekly exercise classes, walks with friends, or daily mindfulness breaks. I think about recognizing when I'm entering into a difficult season and making other parts of life easier or lighter to compensate. And I think about moments of crisis when the best option is to shut everything down and ask for help.

Try this

Let's focus for a moment on predictive or calendar-based maintenance. What are daily or weekly preventative maintenance tasks that you could invite into your system? I often encourage clients to schedule time for a weekly life admin meeting. Is there room for something like that in your life?

Now, looking ahead at an entire year, are there times that are usually hard for you? What predictive maintenance activities could be helpful? In his wonderful book called *Rest*, Alex Soojung-Kim Pang delved into research and determined that the ideal schedule would involve taking a week off every three months. Is that available to you? If not, how close can you get? Can you accommodate a slower schedule or a fallow time every three months?

Imagine a balance beam

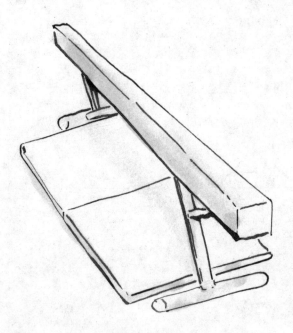

Before we start playing with the idea of a balance beam, let's first talk about streaks. If you want to invite a new behaviour or habit into your life, creating and protecting a streak can be really effective. You do something, put a check on the calendar to show that you've done it, and then if you keep doing that, after a while you'll see a long string of similar checkmarks. You might feel like you've got something worth protecting, and that feeling might be enough to urge you into doing something on a day when otherwise you might not feel like doing it. That feeling kept me exercising throughout the pandemic, so I respect it.

The other feelings associated with streaks that often show up in my therapy office, however, are shame, hopelessness, and frustration. Shame because something got in the way and the streak was broken, which can invite in self-criticism and hugely negative self-talk. I remember one client saying, "This is just more evidence that I screw everything up." Hopelessness because something that's supposed to help you change isn't working for you—so what will? Frustration because sometimes streaks end when other responsibilities of daily life get in the way, and we can end up feeling angry and resentful. The story that shows up might sound something like, "I don't get to have this for myself."

I also see people channelling so much energy and attention into protecting a streak that they lose focus on other important parts of life, like relationships or rest. Any encouragement to hold that streak lightly feels like erasure or betrayal.

It does sound strange and counterproductive to think about holding a streak lightly. I mean, the whole point is to take it seriously enough that it keeps going, right? And here is where the image of a balance beam comes in handy.

Please bear in mind that all of this is imagined because I haven't been on a balance beam in forty years, and I have zero interest in ever getting on one again. In any case, when I envision a gymnast learning a routine on a balance beam, sharpening their skills and learning new tricks, I can easily imagine them falling off. If they're genuinely doing something new, they're going to fall or hop down at some point. Falling off isn't the enemy, and it isn't the end.

In fact, falling off might even be proof that you're trying something interesting and doing something new. We cannot exist permanently in a state of balance or in any state for that matter—joy, pain, inspiration, and so on. The nature of human experience is to move in and out of states. We complicate things by assigning so much judgment to our state changes, even though it's natural and inevitable. In fact, much of our pain comes from resisting or denying this movement. It's interesting to think about what opens up for us if we gently accept and make room for falls when they happen and recognize them as a necessary part of our experience.

When a gymnast falls off a beam, what might happen next? If it's a gentle fall, they might take a moment, stretch, and grab some water. They might talk something through with a coach or a teammate. Then at some point they probably get back on and try again.

If it's a big fall, and there's the possibility of injury, something different might roll out. They could need care and attention. They might need expert help. There might be rare occasions when the fall prompts a re-evaluation and a decision that the balance beam isn't where they want to be. More often, they might take time to rest and heal and then try again.

We can import all of these models into our lives and our practices. If we fall off our own balance beam, perhaps the first questions we can ask ourselves are *How am I feeling? Did this feel like a gentle fall or a big fall? Can I give myself a moment to breathe, to feel the regular floor under my feet? Is there someone like a coach or a friend handy to ground me with connection?* Then, with a gentle curiosity, and if we don't need further tending or time, can we see what it feels like to hop back up?

This discussion reminds me of something I learned when I was working with a wonderful quality improvement group focused on making things better in hospitals (specifically Neonatal Intensive Care Units). If you're working with very small babies, you don't want to mess around, and you REALLY don't want to experiment care-lessly. So how do you introduce positive change? How do you try new things?

The fine people at the Vermont Oxford Network worked a lot with the concept of "Potentially Better Practices," and as healthcare organizations often do, they shortened that term to PBPs. PBPs are things that current knowledge or common sense would suggest are good things to do, but there isn't a lot of evidence related to them. Sometimes there's no evidence because the practice just seems like such an obvious positive move. Do we need evidence to prove that holding babies is good for them or that speaking kindly to cowork-ers or patients creates a better environment? We could have a long debate about this, but in this moment and for our purposes, let's say that evidence helps. When resources are limited and hard choices have to be made, being able to link a practice with a good outcome means that people are more likely to focus attention on that prac-tice and make it a priority. Not everything can be a priority at the same time.

Working with this idea of PBPs gives us a structure or model for introducing practices, for noticing their impact on desired out-comes and then for either integrating them or abandoning them.

What can this look like if we take it out of the hospital and try it in our own lives? It might start with a moment of curiosity. For example, a friend swears by the practice of getting up extremely early and writing for the first hour of the day. Something about that sparks my interest, so I decide to give it a try. Maybe for the first week I really struggle. I sleep through or snooze my alarm. Perhaps one day I experience some success—and perhaps also on that day I find myself running out of steam at 5 p.m., which doesn't work for me.

Historically this is the point where I would abandon the new idea, perhaps before I really had enough evidence to know if it was something that could work for me or not.

But let's name this new practice as a PBP, a potentially better practice. And let's see if we can stick with it a little longer. Can I make one small tweak (just one!) to see if this practice works for me? Maybe I move my alarm farther away from my bed. I could try setting it for 6:30 a.m. instead of 6 a.m. I could try going to bed a little earlier. I could try getting some movement in at that 5 p.m. mark when I'm flagging.

(And in the interest of transparency, I tried working with this practice for a long time, and ultimately decided it didn't work for me. I did learn that I need movement first thing in the morning and to go outside. If I do those things, I have the energy I need for my day. I block off time for writing at the beginning of each week and I work hard to respect those blocks. So even though I didn't adopt this PBP as my own, experimenting with it taught me many important things about what works for me, and I'm happy I committed to looking at this closely.)

What's important here is to (a) make one small change at a time; (b) carry out that change for a good amount of time (let's say at least two weeks); and (c) keep track of what we're experiencing. We often think we will remember what a change feels like and what shifts in our day without writing it down, but that's true for very few people. Most of us need to keep track of our data to be able to make sense of it later. If journaling doesn't appeal to you, create a spreadsheet. If you hate spreadsheets, make a voice note or text a friend. Make a checklist on a dry-erase board or give yourself stickers on a sticker chart.

How does this relate to our balance beam? If we find ourselves falling off a lot, let's not get judgmental but let's be curious. Let's figure out which PBPs we can play with and what small tweaks we can try to help us stay up longer. Let's commit to keeping track. We can treat our data as vitally important information that merits close and respectful attention. And with all the information that we gain from this process of treating our own experiences with respect, we can design the most dazzling routines, execute the most exhilarating maneuvers, and nail those dismounts.

Try this

Let's pick a few areas people often want to make changes in. For now, we'll say relationships, sleep, work, learning, and movement. Does one of those words stand out to you? Write it down.

Now pick one very small PBP you might want to try related to that word. Pick something you're a little curious about that's pretty low stakes. Something like *Text a friend each day*, *Go to bed at 10:30 p.m. each night*, or *Actually take my vitamins instead of leaving them on the counter*. Write it down too.

Try your PBP for at least two weeks. Keep track of when you do it and what you notice. If you miss a day, write down what got in the way. At the end of two weeks, ask yourself if you want to keep going. Whatever you decide, take a moment to celebrate. You just executed some amazing tricks on the balance beam by investing time and attention in your own wellbeing.

Imagine a ladder

I hate heights. HATE them. I've been up the Empire State Building twice because my kids wanted to go, and I don't think they appreciate how heroic that was. I get a little shaky in office towers or tall condo buildings, and if I have to walk over a bridge, I am very, very careful not to look down. So, when I was searching for an image to help people unpack their complicated feelings related to being stuck in a situation they can't change, a ladder came to mind.

Imagine that someone grabs you by the back of the neck and plunks you on the top rung of a very, very tall ladder. You've got nothing to hang onto, and while you would love to be back on the ground again, you can't climb down just yet. You have to stay on that ladder.

Can you feel the vigilance creeping into your body, the tension in your stomach and your legs? Is your heart racing? Is your breath a little irregular or is your jaw tight?

But you can't come down off the ladder right now. That's not available to you just yet. But what if you come down just one rung? Maybe one more? What if now you're at a place where you can hang onto something? You can take a deep breath. Maybe your heart can slow down, and maybe you can start feeling a little bit more like yourself.

While one rung down isn't the same as solid ground, it probably feels a little bit better. Focusing on just one rung at a time reduces the pressure we feel, and we realize we don't have to fix everything or get over everything right in that exact moment. We just need to come down one rung on our ladder.

What can we take from this? If our nervous systems are revved up because we're in a difficult situation that we can't get out of, it's okay that we're yearning for it to be over. But while we're waiting for it to be over, what can we do to come down our ladders? What can we do to tend to our nervous systems so that we don't feel like our bodies are caught up in vigilance, or that all our energy has to be focused on keeping our balance in the most challenging position? Living in the upper register of our nervous system is exhausting and destructive. What moves can we make? When we don't have control, can we still exercise some agency?

I found myself using this image with parents in the hospital, and with nurses and other clinicians. We explored so many varied tricks and techniques that resonated for different people. We talked about movement and breathing and connection and laughter. We discussed Instagram cat videos, Jolly Rancher candies, really luxurious hand cream, and beaded bracelets you can run through your fingers. We shared favourite scents, songs, and Doritos flavours. Everyone came up with a slightly different toolbox filled with go-to strategies to help them come down their ladders one rung at a time.

It's important to notice that what helps one person feel safe and good may not help someone else. Some of my nurse friends read the goriest, most disgusting crime novels in order to relax; those books would have had me screaming in the middle of the night. So start building your toolbox you need to centre your own experience and pay close attention to what feels good for you.

Take care of your body first. If you're not in a place where your physical self is safe, there's not much the rest of you can do to feel secure. Other strategies will be playing a stop-gap role until you can get yourself to a place that feels like it's safe enough.

Think small. If you imagine climbing a ladder, it's much easier if the rungs are fairly close together and you don't have to haul your-self up over huge gaps. A weekend away might be wonderful, but it's expensive and not always doable. What's something that gives you an echo or a small taste of that feeling that can happen in ten seconds?

You might want to think back on places where you felt safe, or people who cared for you, and notice what memories show up, and what actions might attach to those memories. Is there anything you can bring into the present moment that might evoke those feelings from the past?

I can't help but feel there's a delicious sort of resistance caught up in this process; it's a reclamation or assertion of power. There is so much we have no control over, which can make us feel hopeless and helpless. What might it feel like to know that, even in our hardest moments, we can harness our own knowledge of ourselves to get to where we need to be on our ladder?

Try this

A colleague introduced me to the wonderful work of Deb Dana, whose Autonomic Ladder model is beautifully comprehensive and grounded in Polyvagal Theory (developed by Stephen Borges). Deb's ladder stands as a model for our nervous system. At the top is where we feel safe and secure. (I'm guessing Deb isn't afraid of heights, if she puts the safe state at the top of her ladder.) In the middle is a stressed and anxious state; we are mobilizing for action, perhaps moving toward fight or flight. At the bottom of the ladder, we are in a state of immobilization or shutdown. Think of a small animal curling up and playing dead.

Deb's invitation is to find ways to move yourself up your ladder by identifying ventral vagal anchors. These anchors are people, places, actions, and moments that help you feel safe and connected. She also coined the term "glimmers," which are signs of safety that we find in the world around us. Functionally, glimmers are the opposite of triggers, which are signs of danger. We may be more used to scanning for signs of danger, but if we accept the invitation to begin looking for glimmers as well we can give ourselves a powerful yet gentle tool to help keep us in our window of tolerance and remain in a regulated and connected state.

Do you know what your anchors and glimmers are?

Think of times when you felt safe, joyful, or connected. Who was there? Where were you? What were you doing? When have you felt truly seen and heard? What did that feel like?

Make a list of activities, people, and sensory experiences that evoke these feelings of safety and connection.

Imagine a dance floor

Let's say you're out and about at some sort of event and suddenly your song comes on. The best song! You don't wait for anyone else but just run right out to the dance floor. A young and joyful part of you takes over and is having the best time—until you catch a glimpse of someone standing off to the side, not moving, watching you and the other dancers with a stony face. A judgy face. Maybe there are a few judgy faces lined up. Those judgmental gazes take you right out of yourself, and your joy dims. That young part of you suddenly gets quiet and disappears. You can't feel foolish and joyful at the same time.

I hate that feeling. To be made to feel ridiculous for trying something or enjoying something leaves us in such a vulnerable and lonely place. And it can happen in all sorts of locations—in the classroom, on a sports field, at work, or in a relationship. I've seen it happen in the therapy room, where one partner in a couple is trying to engage in the process and the other is hanging out on the sidelines, greeting all efforts with contempt.

What's so painful about this dynamic, and what can we do about it?

Let's start with the pain. If I'm trying something new, having an emotional experience, or doing something that's hard for me, I might be feeling vulnerable. And when I'm vulnerable and someone else is disrespectful of that, I can feel unsafe. My human desire to experience something has somehow blown up in my face. I think that's what it can feel like for a person who's trying to be honest about their emotions, trying to connect with a beloved partner, and then experiencing a splash back of ridicule. Or a person who's learning to dance and sees someone rolling their eyes as they attempt a new move.

What helps me sometimes, if I'm on a dance floor (or in a swimming pool or on a soccer field—adjust the metaphor as needed to suit your situation), is to give myself a pause, a breath, and an invitational reminder that there's a reason I'm where I am at that particular moment. Chances are the reason I'm there is not to be focused on what someone else thinks at the expense of my own experience. I can ground or centre myself by asking *What is the work of this moment*? If the answer is to dance, I'll dance.

Then if I find my mind hamster-wheeling about that person on the sidelines (what was their PROBLEM anyway?), I might try to use a lens of compassion and wonder why they're on the sidelines instead of enjoying themselves with the rest of the dancers.

The answers come more easily then. They don't know how. They hate not knowing how to do things. Maybe not knowing hasn't been safe for them in the past. They've been taught that dancing is silly or bad, which is so sad. Or they've been taught that you're only allowed to do things you're good at, which is impossible. Maybe they genuinely don't understand that other people enjoy dancing and moving their bodies, and maybe they fear what they don't understand and seek to devalue it. And maybe underneath the contempt there's a secret longing to join in, but it's blocked by all the fear.

There are all kinds of reasons why someone might be hanging out by a dance floor being an asshole, and none of them have anything to do with the dancers.

So, to the people on the sidelines: it's okay to be there! There's no rush and no pressure. You may think you don't know how to dance. You have choices. You can risk trying it out, moving a bit carefully, following the lead of others around you. You can stay where you are. You could take lessons if you like, to turn down the volume on that *I don't know how* message. You can leave and find something to do that you really like, although I hope one day you'll try again. But please know this: there are better ways for you to spend your time than hanging out on the edge of a dance floor making fun of people who are willing to try.

When I was working through this metaphor with a friend, she burst out laughing and said, "Do you remember that guy?! The one at the bar who was so wild with his arms and knocked over the drinks tray? How does he fit in here?"

Oh right—THAT guy. I think he fits in here as well, and this is a nice example of how flexible these metaphors can be. He was absolutely and enthusiastically showing up on the dance floor, but he wasn't paying any attention to the people around him. He was having a solo experience in a communal context. And he didn't really deserve our ridicule either, but perhaps a gentle word to watch where his elbows were going would have been helpful.

Let's jump back for a moment into the role of dancer. We're enjoying ourselves, we're laughing, we're watching our elbows, we're connecting, and then we look at the person on the sidelines. We might have big thoughts or feelings about what they're doing. If we see overt signs that they're being judgmental or contemptuous, that's one thing. But what if they're just standing there, quietly watching?

In those moments, maybe we send a message of inclusion by creating a space for them to come into, beckoning them in with open arms, or simply smiling. We might be tempted to just drag them in, but unless we know them REALLY well, it's unlikely that's going to work.

What probably serves us best in those moments is to assume the best of the person on the sidelines. Maybe they're learning, maybe they're shy, maybe they have a good reason to not participate in that moment. We might feel some sadness that they're not getting to have the experience we're having, but it's their right to choose the sidelines, even if that's a choice we couldn't imagine ourselves making. We can refocus our energy from the observer to our own experience. Our song is not going to last forever. Let's enjoy it while we can.

Try this

If you notice you fall at times into the protective but destructive grip of contempt, you might want to look up John and Julie Gottman, who have done transformative work in the realm of relationships and connection. Of all the things that can damage relationships, they name contempt as the most dangerous.

They've also identified the antidote to contempt, which has two layers. The first is taking a moment to identify what longing or need hides behind the contemptuous statement or behaviour and to express it clearly to the other person. The other layer is to cultivate a culture of appreciation in your relationship by regularly sharing gratitude, being kind, and showing appreciation for the other person with words and actions.

Is there someone in your orbit who brings up feelings of contempt in you? It could be someone close to you or someone at arm's length, like a community figure or celebrity. Can you identify what it is about them that makes you feel these strong feelings? You may notice an unmet need of your own surfacing. For example, you may dislike how someone seeks out attention, and that may be connected to your own feelings of invisibility. Or you may see them be-having in a way that's contrary to one of your own cherished values, and you just can't understand that.

Maybe imagine that person as a younger version of themselves, stepping awkwardly out on the dance floor. You can also envision them in some other vulnerable context—like a hospital waiting room or waiting for a bus in the rain. See if you notice feelings of compassion surfacing.

Now, see if there is anything at all you can notice about that person that you appreciate. It can be a big or a small characteristic, but it's something you can genuinely say something positive about. Do you notice more compassion showing up? Does that sharp contempt feel a little dulled? The goal here isn't to turn this person into your favourite but to be able to see them as a full and complex human being.

Imagine a frozen lake

This metaphor grew out of the previous one; I was talking with a client who just couldn't imagine himself on a dance floor but could imagine himself on a hockey rink. He remembered learning to skate on a frozen lake and how they tested the ice for safety before anyone could venture out.

That made me think about what it feels like in friendships or other relationships when we're venturing out, not sure if the ice is strong enough or not. We may have had terrifying experiences in the past when we thought the ice would hold us, but we fell through. We may have, in fact, never experienced a sense of safety on the ice at all. Our first relationships in our family of origin may have taught us that ice is never to be trusted, and any time we're out there we're so vigilant that we can feel it in our entire body. We're listening for sounds of cracking and watching for signs of breaking, and all that watching and listening gives us no time to just be.

What we're really talking about here is attachment and how

our first relationships (and the ones that follow) contribute to our felt sense of safety with other people. When I talk about attachment with clients, I lean heavily on the work of researchers like John Bowlby and Mary Ainsworth, who developed their ideas about parent-child relationships into what we now know as Attachment Theory. I'm also inspired by the work of psychologist Stan Tatkin, who uses evocative metaphors to help people understand their own attachment style.

There are three main attachment styles, which are secure, avoidant, and anxious. Securely attached people feel safe, trusted, valued, and understood in relationships. They can move through disagreements or ruptures without losing themselves. They had predictable, emotionally responsive caregivers growing up. People with avoidant attachment struggle with emotional closeness. They may have had emotionally unresponsive or unavailable caregivers growing up, they may prize independence, and they may associate or confuse emotional closeness with weakness or neediness. Anxious attachment comes from inconsistent or unpredictable caregivers, and can turn into fear of abandonment, low self-esteem, and a real hunger for connection. People with anxious attachment can often experience bursts of deep anger when they feel the relationship is threatened in any way because they experience that threat so personally.

Let's get these different attachment types out on the lake. The secure types find it easy to start skating and recover quickly from any falls. If they get their feet wet, they'll get sorted out and back on the ice, and they may have a hard time understanding anyone who isn't having the same kind of good time that they are.

For those avoidant types who find relationships hard and who maybe have never felt truly safe in a relationship, they may never want to venture out onto the icy lake. If they do, they might retreat at the first sign that something might be off. "The sun's too bright—the ice is going to melt!" And off they go, back to the side of the lake or the safety of the car, where they'll pull out their phone and distract themselves from whatever's unfolding in front of them.

For those with an anxious attachment pattern, they might be skating around in circles trying to entice their partners onto the lake. If their partners ignore them, they might get very angry. They might start trying to drag their partners out, they might take their own skates off and hurl them into the snowbank in frustration. Or, if they get very angry, they might even start jumping up and down on the ice to prove that it's strong enough. Sometimes they jump so much they break through. It could be a cry for attention or a desperate need to force an end to an experience that's so painful. Maybe it feels better in that moment to destroy it all than to be abandoned. Then of course if they do break through, there's no more skating to be done that day, and they're wet and cold into the bargain.

Let's stand for a minute on the shore of the lake, and think about what we need to feel safe about venturing out. There might be some signs we're looking for that tell us the ice is solid. What might indicate to us that a relationship could hold us? The things that movies and books say we should look for might not be so useful here.

Drama, fire, and passion make for wonderful moments on a screen but don't necessarily contribute to stability, solidity, or living well day to day. We might have to turn to other markers.

Words like caring, honesty, fairness, transparency, awareness, and accountability might show up here. I've come to realize that the most important thing to me in a relationship (any relationship—my primary relationship, my friendships, my working relationships) is that people treat me with some care. Carelessness feels dangerous. People don't need to be perfect, and there's always room for mistakes, but if we can work through these ruptures while still showing we care, that means everything to me.

Those of us with avoidant tendencies might need to get a little brave about sharing what's going on for us. Sometimes we might need to claim time for ourselves, which might sound something like, "I'm really overwhelmed right now and need an hour to connect with myself. Then I'll come find you, and we can work this out." (Notice how there's a time commitment here? That's really important. Leaving people hanging, especially those with anxious attachment, causes pain.) It's sort of like saying, "I really don't feel like skating, but I'll try it for twenty minutes. Then I'll wait for you in the cabin." That's how we can find a balance between our own needs and those of the other, and that's how we can exhibit care both for ourselves and for the other.

Those with anxious attachment, especially when in relationship with avoidant types, might want to focus on their own experience in the moment. Am I skating because I really want to be skating, or am I assigning skating (or any other activity) a relational importance that maybe it doesn't need to carry? If someone doesn't want to skate, are they rejecting me, or do I have a choice about framing it like that?

If I find myself jumping on the ice, really putting it to the test, can I bring awareness to the moment and ask myself why I'm doing this? Why do I need to set up tests in the relationship? Is there another more direct way of getting the information I need? Can I have a direct conversation? Can I ask for what I need and work with the response I get?

Let's look at a real-life moment where this sort of dynamic shows up frequently. Many people in couples therapy talk about their deep disappointment around gift-giving. They hope that their partner will choose something for them that makes them feel understood and loved. Instead, they get something that doesn't feel like a fit, and they feel misunderstood and devastated.

In one of these discussions, I asked if they gave each other lists of what they would like as gifts. One partner grimaced and said, "That's so unromantic! People should know! If they don't know, then they aren't paying attention."

I asked, "Is there another reason why someone might get it wrong? Could they be nervous about giving gifts? Could they be afraid because of past experiences when they got it wrong and so now trying feels risky? And more to the point—how is this working for you? The way you're doing it now?"

The answer was that it wasn't working at all. And while they had named sharing lists or communicating openly about what they wanted as "unromantic," the discontent and disconnection that happened after every holiday was the farthest thing from romance one could imagine.

Maybe we don't need these little tests. Maybe we can just communicate honestly and openly about what we want. The joyful connection we seek might then happen, not because someone made a lucky guess and got it right but because two people were able to have a direct conversation. They heard each other, took it seriously, and acted on it.

Another thought for those angry anxious types skating around on the iced-over lake: I understand why you feel the need to test the ice again and again. You want connection, you've been hurt before, and you're trying all sorts of strategies to get the relationship you want and to feel like you can trust it. It's also true that if you keep testing the ice with greater and greater force, at some point it will break. You might then think, "Well—that's my proof! It couldn't hold me." But everything has its breaking point, even really thick ice. So please pay attention to what you're doing to test your ice. A few jumps up and down? Makes sense. Using a jackhammer? Driving a truck out onto the lake? At some point, you'll go right through. Please ask yourself, *Why does the broken ice feel safer for me? What can I do to help myself feel safe enough on the ice without all the testing and retesting?*

One way of making sure our relational ice is thick enough to hold us is to keep flooding it with generosity. This is true of any system, whether we're talking about romantic partnerships, friendships, or workplaces. Every time we let someone know that we see them, we appreciate them, we think they matter, and that we take their interests and wellbeing seriously, we're adding layers and making that relationship feel more solid. If you're feeling disconnected in a relationship it might feel strange or even scary to consider putting more generosity and kindness into that particular system, but the amazing thing is that generosity usually begets more generosity.

Sometimes people do this with their partners, friends, or coworkers without mentioning that they're doing it intentionally, and it can still work! I think, though, there's a beautiful benefit to be gained by being upfront about what we're doing.

We can say something like, "I've been thinking about how I can show you how important you are to me more regularly. You might notice that I'm more open about things I appreciate about you, and that I'm doing more small things for you. I'd love it if you could join me in this experiment. I think it would help us feel more connected." And then we can figure out together what this could look like.

Sometimes it takes a while for people to be able to show up for the experiment. Sometimes they genuinely can't show up at all for it because they carry such a burden of relational trauma that connection actually feels too dangerous for them. They may not participate in good faith or may turn away from it entirely. This may bring up some difficult questions about the sustainability of the relationship if all the generosity is coming from one party.

Often, however, when someone is brave enough to take on the risk of putting generosity into the system, of turning a hose on and adding layers to that frozen lake, it emboldens others to join and to participate more fully. I love the idea that one person's courage to be openhearted and generous could lead to a frozen lake full of skaters, twirling and toppling and having a wonderful time.

Try this

To bring some awareness to our own dynamics in painful relational moments, we need to have a sense of our attachment style. There are many books you can read about this, quizzes you can take online, and of course you can always explore this with a therapist. For now, we can get the ball rolling with a few simple questions.

The first of the following questions was inspired by the Adult Attachment Interview, a powerful instrument designed by psychologist Mary Main that helps adults understand both their past and current experiences with attachment. The last three are questions I often explore because they bring up such powerful stories.

1. When you were ill, injured, or upset as a child, what would you do? What would happen?

2. When you made a mistake as a child, what would happen next? If you made a small mistake (like spilling a glass of water) what would happen? What about a bigger mistake?

3. Who do you turn to for support or comfort now? Do you feel comfortable asking for help?

4. Why do your relationships end? Do you feel the other person is demanding too much? Do you feel your needs are never being met?

These answers will give you great information about your attachment patterns by clarifying which needs of yours were met and which were missed. You may notice that you routinely did not get the care you needed or that you were treated as a nuisance or a problem when you needed something. Maybe someone laughed at your distress. Hopefully someone was kind. Maybe there wasn't anyone there at all. Maybe you didn't feel there was room to make mistakes, or you felt afraid or judged. These questions can be painful to explore, but they'll help you understand why certain experiences are hard for you to have in the present moment, and they might nudge you toward a fuller understanding of your attachment pattern.

Imagine a mountain

Mountains loom large in our geographies and in our imagina-tions. They can represent goals (both attainable and unattainable), certainties, obstacles, significant moments, obligations, or power. Right now, we're going to use this image in a very specific way; we're going to imagine that someone we love is lost somewhere halfway up the mountain.

They are distressed and confused, which doesn't surprise us at all because they're lost on a mountainside! What do we do next, once we've heard them shouting for help or crying out in fear and worry?

Do we stand at the bottom of the mountain and try to convince them that they aren't lost? That their fear or worry is foolish and un-necessary? That their anger or frustration is silly? That, in fact, they are standing right next to us and all is well? Do we describe to them exactly what to do to get down? Would we shout something like "Take twenty steps forward, then turn to the right and take that path for ten minutes, and then . . . "? Would we yell at them with irritation or rage in our voice in that moment for getting lost, and tell them that if they'd only listened to us, they wouldn't be up there shivering alone on the mountain? Would we treat them like an inconvenience?

I don't think we would. I hope we wouldn't. I hope that we would do all we could to come to where they are on the mountain, be with them, and take care of them.

I use this image when my rational mind, my intellect, is telling me to meet someone else's emotions with reason or denial or annoyance. When someone shows up with big, complex feelings, whether it's a family member, a friend, or a client, if my first move is to tell them that they don't need to feel what they're feeling, it's just not going to work. I might not understand why they're feeling what they're feeling. I might have opinions about their feelings. I might remember times when I felt the same way and just pushed through and got on with things. If I respond with that advice, what might happen next?

Most likely they'll feel unheard, unseen, and like they're all alone, stranded on the mountain. They might realize, either implicitly or explicitly, that I'm privileging my own discomfort with feelings over their experience.

It's something we've been encouraged to do and that has been done to us many times. Can you remember a time when you were told that you weren't feeling what you were feeling? Or that whatever you were feeling was wrong? We do this all the time to children. "Don't be sad! You have nothing to be sad about!" "Why are you angry? You should feel lucky!" "Don't tell me you're still crying about that! That's so silly. That happened a week ago!" So many ways we're told that we shouldn't feel what we feel.

It doesn't stop in childhood, of course. In adulthood we get told to smile, told to "think positive," or warned that our emotions are un-professional. Our loved ones and other people around us make it quite clear what emotions are welcome and what emotions are not welcome. The more that happens to us, the more we do it to other people. Part of that urge might be hidden resentment (why should they get to take up so much space when I never get to?) or protective inclinations (they are going to be so vulnerable if they show every-one what they're feeling!).

If we can hit pause for a second and think about this person in front of us who, emotionally speaking, is stranded up on a moun-tain, and stop judging their emotion and just see it for what it is, what happens next?

There's a beautiful therapeutic model called Emotion Focused Therapy, developed by Sue Johnson and Leslie Greenberg and often used with couples or families. Instead of rushing to solve or erase or deny someone's feelings, this model encourages curiosity. With EFT, we spend time exploring and acknowledging the emotion. We validate it and help name it. We invest time into demonstrating to the other person that we're paying attention and doing our best to understand. Depending on the situation, we may apologize or take responsibility for our part in a dynamic. We clarify the emotional need and then do what we can to meet it. Only after we've invested this amount of time into being curious about the emotion and being with the emotion can we make any kind of move toward problem solving. What's interesting about this approach is that often the focus on understanding and connection means that there's not all that much problem-solving left to do. It's sort of like how we might search for our person up on the mountain, be with them where they are, show them some attention and care, and then they can find their own way down.

Let's take a moment now to shift our perspective. Now we are the ones lost on the mountain. We had all the big feelings, we felt afraid or angry or unseen, and our person came to meet us on the mountain. They found us! They listened to us! We are no longer alone. What happens next?

We may be so overwhelmed in the moment that we feel stuck in noticing our own experience, and that's okay. My hope though is that with a bit of time, we can take a breath, and we can notice what they've done. We can appreciate the work, the effort, that they've expended on our behalf.

Coming to find us on the mountain may not be an easy thing for them to do. They may never have had help themselves finding their way down. This might be unfamiliar territory for them. Even if it is familiar, they may be tired themselves. Do we have an awareness of what other mountains they may have been climbing that day? And yet they set off to find us, and here they are. How can we let them know we see and appreciate them? What might it feel like to say, even in the midst of our own regulating process, that we are grateful for how they've shown up? This isn't about apologizing; it's about valuing the work our person has done for us and making sure they know that we see the work and we see them.

Try this

If you're interested in trying an emotion-focused approach with people close to you, here are five steps to remember (courtesy of clinical psychologist Adele Lafrance).

1. Attend to and acknowledge the emotion. Let the person know you see them and hear them. (And while you're at it, pay attention to your own emotions—and maybe take a deep breath or two.)

2. Name the emotion. Help the person name what it is that they're feeling.

3. Validate the emotion. Let them know it's okay for them to feel what they feel. This can be tough! Remember you're validating the emotion, not any behaviour.

4. Identify and meet the need. Every emotion needs something. For example, anger wants respect, loneliness wants connection. If you're not sure, you can offer a hug or even your silent presence.

5. Problem-solving. Often, we rush through to this step, but there is no rush! In fact, if you don't hurry through the first four steps, the person may solve their own problem by the time you get to this point. You can offer your assistance, and it's okay if they don't want it. You've established that you're a safe person for them to talk to, so even if they don't accept your help at that moment, they know who they can come to if they change their mind or need support in the future.

Imagine a garden

Let's come down off the mountain and into a wide flat field. If we look around, we'll see that the field is divided into different plots or gardens; some are contained by split rail fences, others surrounded by sweet flowers, and some have nothing around them or in them at all.

We walk up to one plot and realize that this is for us; perhaps our name is on the gate or perhaps we just know. It looks and feels familiar. What do we see when we look at it from the outside? What do we see when we walk through the gate? We're not concerned in this moment how it may have looked before or what it might be like in the future. It may once have been a formal garden with sharp-edged hedges. We might be hoping for a glorious wild tangle or well-organized rows of vegetables. For now, we're just curious about what we see in front of us.

We might notice that there are beautiful trees and blooms all around the edges, but the interior of the plot is empty and neglected.

All the attention has been focused on what people passing by can see, and there's been no time or energy left over for the inside. It's dusty, but if we bend and dig a little, we realize just underneath the surface the soil is still rich and dark.

One client shared that there was nothing growing in his plot at all; instead, there were facades or false fronts surrounding his land, so that it looked lush and inviting from the outside. Behind those false fronts was an arid vacancy. Other clients have imagined plots full of vegetables and grains that other people come to harvest, leaving the land trampled and tired.

What these imaginings reveal is a core story that we carry, a story about our big pain or our big pattern. These core stories might sound something like, "There's nothing worthwhile inside me that anyone would want to see" or "My value is in what I create for other people, and if I don't produce that I won't be loved." These stories are neither true nor false, though they are intimately connected to our own histories of being loved or not loved, and seen or not seen. They are in some ways above truth; what I mean by that is I don't think there's much point in arguing with them, at least not before they've been identified and understood.

Once we name our core story, our big fear, our big pain, our repeating pattern, we can open the gate to a small experiment. For example, let's say I've noticed that within my garden the edges receive most of the attention, and that's where I feel safest or where my efforts feel most appreciated. That helps me name that I feel safest on the outskirts or on the edges generally, and the thought of moving into the centre feels uncomfortable or frightening.

Perhaps I start by imagining moving into the interior of this small plot of land and sitting down. I can dig my hands down into the dirt and see what it feels like. Maybe I see that the dirt needs some attention or some water. I'm in no rush; it might not be the season for planting but rather for preparation. At some point that will change, and I can start trying different plants to see what grows well in the inner heart of this garden.

My aunt and uncle have the most glorious garden that inspires me every time I see it. It takes tons of work, and I have often wondered how they know what will grow and how to tend it. My uncle says there's no mystery to it; they try planting something in one corner and either it works or it doesn't. If it doesn't, they'll move it and try again. They've learned a lot over the years and they're always willing to learn more. Their garden is a playful labour, an imaginative experiment, a daily invitation to show up and pay attention. While it's incredibly beautiful, there is no one moment when everything is in perfect bloom. One part might be exploding while another part is dying.

Seeing their garden makes me think about what it might feel like to pay that kind of loving attention to my own imagined garden plot, to accept that not everything will be in bloom at the same time, and to try out different plantings in the centre, to see what suits the soil and what doesn't. I don't have to build a monument to outlast me, something with a value connected to its continued existence. I can live, instead, in a state of loving experimentation, learning about what flourishes in each season and in this soil and enjoying each bloom as it arrives.

Try this

This metaphor lends itself beautifully to playing with different art therapy techniques. Grab some markers or paints and sketch out your garden plot on paper. Think about what brings you joy and connection—these could be people, pets, sounds, activities, tastes, or objects.

You can imagine them as different elements of a garden (flowers, vines, vegetables, etc.) and experiment with where you put them. Notice how you assign space to different elements and what feels like it belongs together.

Next, think about what you might want more of in your life. Are there goals you want to accomplish or experiences you want to invite in? Find a place to plant these as well.

If you don't like drawing, you can experiment with collage, or you can write a description and add colourful flourishes. The point is to be playful and go with what feels good without thinking about it too much. My guess is you'll be surprised and delighted by what shows up.

Imagine some scaffolding

When I think of scaffolding, I picture a building in need of some attention, surrounded by metal and wood. While the building is getting what it needs, the scaffolding stays. Sometimes it's just for a few weeks, sometimes it's for years, and then eventually it's no longer needed, and it goes away. If the building ever needs attention again, the scaffolding comes back up. It's not permanent, but it's always available.

This image comes up a lot when working with people who are in the middle of a crisis or other significant life transformation. I talk about it with parents whose babies are in the NICU, with people approaching retirement, with people experiencing chronic illness, or with couples figuring out major relationship issues.

The core message is pretty much always the same: in the midst of a crisis, when you're feeling really lost and you're not sure what to do next, it's worth going back to basics. You get to decide what your basics are. You get to name what practices and behaviours make up the boards and supports of your scaffolding. You might identify some by remembering what helped you during other hard times, or you might experiment with what's been helpful for other people in your situation. The point is to keep it simple and focus on what grounds and supports you. A crisis isn't the moment to throw lots of complex new possibilities into the mix.

If people feel very stuck with this piece, I often suggest looking at these four elements: sleep, movement, connection, and nutrition. I'll focus first on sleep because I think it's so foundational. If you're exhausted, you're going to find it hard to put energy toward any other kind of change. If your sleep is shaky, what can be brought in to support this part of your life?

I'm reminded of a conversation I would often have with parents before they took their babies home from the NICU. I loved sitting down with them to have an open discussion about sleep—not their baby's sleep, which of course everyone was focusing on, but *their* sleep. How were they going to work together to make sure each person got enough sleep so that everyone could cope? If one person went without decent sleep for more than two nights in a row, did they have a plan to address that? We might talk about buying earplugs and each parent getting protected sleep time or calling in trusted family members or friends to take shifts with the baby so that a parent could rest. The point was to take a moment to talk about it, identify it as important, and come up with some strategies ahead of time because problem-solving when you're already exhausted is impossible. All I did was open up the conversation, and the parents themselves chose the methods and strategies that worked for them within the context of their own lives.

It's good to remember that you can choose the kinds of changes you invite in, in the realm of sleep or in any other part of life. You can talk to an expert, you can make a list of changes to try, and you can ask for help from people around you. It often makes sense to make one small change at a time, just as we discussed in the section about the balance beam. You want to be clear about what exactly is helping you, and it also makes sense to track what you're doing, because we often think we'll remember all the details of what we've experienced and when it happened, but our brain doesn't always cooperate. Using an app or jotting down details in a journal will help you notice what changes are happening and what actions they're connected to.

What you're looking for is a small test of change, a small move-able piece, that you can put into place in your daily routine. You can step toward this with an experimental lens, treating yourself as a curious scientist looking at your life. You're not trying to force a pattern; you're doing small experiments and being open and curi-ous about what happens next. You could also imagine a huge, tan-gled knot of yarn; you aren't going to start yanking the whole thing around because that's not going to help. You'll look for a small piece that looks like an end and start by working with that gently.

If you're looking at movement, the first step doesn't have to be training for a marathon. It might be going on a five-minute morning walk every day or doing a short exercise video during a work break. If you'd like to feel more connected with others, you might think about someone you haven't been in touch with who you generally feel good about talking to, and you might send them a text. If you want to see how you'd feel if you ate a bit differently, perhaps focus on changing one meal a day to start off with or try meal planning for one week, and see what kinds of feelings and experiences show up.

I think of one client who first began working with me when she was in the middle of a deep crisis of grief. No part of life felt like it was working, and she felt unmoored in the midst of all she was experiencing. We gently looked at what small promises she could make and keep to herself, not in service of erasing or "fixing" what she was going through, but to give her some scaffolding to help her days make sense. Many months after we began our work, she shared with me that her heart had dropped when I had first mentioned looking at movement. "I thought you were going to tell me to exercise, and I was going to hang up right then!" she said. "But then you asked if I thought I could go outside for a couple of minutes in the morning, and I realized that you understood how hard things were right then, and I also realized I could try that." It ended up being a core daily practice for her; she felt it made her day "2 percent better," and when you're carrying such a heavy emotional load, 2 percent matters.

My own experience with movement feels similar to this client's story. For most of my life I was a reluctant exerciser; I'd always been a terrible athlete and associated anything even vaguely related to athletics with failure. "Good for others but not for me" summed up my stance. I tried things now and then, out of a sense of obligation, but nothing stuck. Then, during the pandemic I realized I needed to invite in some more structure for my own wellbeing, and morning movement became a cornerstone of my day. Everything else was stuck, but my body wasn't.

I'm thinking of another experience with movement that I found upsetting at the time, but now I hold it with a very different understanding. When my first daughter was in the NICU, we had some terrible days when we weren't sure if she was going to live. One night I found myself so gripped with fear and exhaustion that I felt I couldn't walk. I was at home and had to get myself up the stairs. I sank to my knees and crawled up the stairs. There was something so reassuring, so regulating about this movement, and I kept crawling around for a bit. I remember wondering if this is what pilgrims on a pilgrimage feel like, allowing their faith to be metabolized through movement. Then I got caught by an image of what I was doing and thought *I'm going insane*. The deep reassurance I had felt was instantly replaced by deep fear.

Now, many years later, I've learned enough about somatic therapy and how movements like crawling can soothe or reset our nervous system to understand that my body was actually being kind to me in that moment. It was an outside fear that blocked me from receiving that kindness. I would handle it much differently now.

Perhaps this is why gentle movement can be so important

for people experiencing deep grief or suffering. Our minds can't make sense of the terrible things that have been happening, and we feel trapped with our thoughts about the reality of what we've experienced. We can't push back against that stuckness with our thoughts, but we can with our bodies. Our bodies, doing whatever kind of movement they can in that moment, can open the door for our minds to follow.

A few weeks ago, I was discussing this idea of scaffolding with a friend, who wondered where art might fit into this. She's a deeply artistic and sensitive person who turns to art in her most difficult moments, and her question felt important. Two thoughts came up in response. The first is that art, or anything else that gives us delight, could belong in the connection domain. Delight is essential fuel that pushes us toward connection with others, with the world around us, and with ourselves. I think of Mary Ainsworth and her transformative work on attachment between parents and babies. Not only did she identify "moments of delight" as key building blocks of attachment, but she recognized that parents had to experience delight in their own lives in order to find it with their children.

The second thought is that this is your scaffolding, and you get to add whatever pieces you need. Whatever practice, whatever moment feels important to you, gets to be there. The one caveat I have is that I hope you don't overload yourself and that you leave space in your day for life to happen, for things to get in the way, and for rest. Apart from that, you're the general contractor here, and you're in charge of what you build.

Now let's turn to the "how" of building. Personally, I find if I take a scaffolding approach to my mornings, the rest of the day rolls out better, or perhaps I just have more capacity to deal with what comes. If I do a bit of exercise, take time to review my day and write down some priorities and intentions, and have a breakfast that feels and tastes good, I can ride that wave of energy for quite some time. I generally organize my mornings for outflow or producing/doing, and my afternoons for inflow, which might look like reading, listening to podcasts, or meeting up with other people.

Another moment that benefits from attention is bedtime. If we take a moment to think about the next day, to organize a few pieces of the next morning as a gift to ourselves, it can help us start the next day with a more open mindset. Of course, we may not always have the power to organize our whole day the way we want to, because that's just not how life works. We can generally bring some choice and intention to bear on how we begin and end it.

The other interesting piece of this metaphor is that scaffolding is not meant to be there forever. A practice that serves us well in crisis may become rigidity or lack of flexibility once the time of crisis passes. We might learn that something that we adopted as a crisis measure is something we want to have as a daily practice, or we might find that we don't need that practice in the same way as our life shifts and changes around us. Our own systems, bodies, feelings, and thoughts will give us the evidence we need to decide what can go and what can stay.

Try this

If you are finding it hard to identify a scaffolding piece to experiment with, one small move can bring in huge positive shifts, and I would love for you to try it. Go outside every day before 10 a.m. for at least ten minutes. You can do some movement, or you can just stand out there. It doesn't matter if it's raining or snowing, although if there's no natural light at all the positive impact won't be quite as powerful. But go anyway. Go every day. See what happens. You might notice a boost in energy, a shift in mood, or an improvement in your sleep. You won't know until you try.

Imagine a bright light

This is a fun thought experiment to do with yourself; just remember that there are no right or wrong answers. We're just exploring!

First, imagine that you're somewhere completely surrounded by dark. Then imagine the flare of a bright light turning on. Then you hear the words, "And now on with the show!"

Where are you?

What are you doing?

When I explore this with clients, so many different images and ideas show up. Often people imagine that they're on a stage, about to put on a show. Sometimes there's an accompanying feeling of anxiety, a worry that they're not going to be good enough or that they're not ready. Every once in a while there's excitement. "This is what I've been waiting for! Finally, I get a chance to show what I can do!"

Many people (including myself) imagine that they're in an audience. I love musical theatre, so I notice myself feeling happy and excited, ready to see talented people do their thing. Sometimes people notice a feeling of disappointment, because they're in the audience but would rather be on stage. Sometimes they feel stuck watching something that they don't like.

A couple of months ago, a client placed themselves in a new spot. They were a stagehand ready to haul the curtain up. They felt anxiety because they felt pressure to get it right, and they also noticed satisfaction that they were about to be a part of something interesting, and relief that they were behind the scenes.

Sometimes it makes sense where people place themselves based on their past experiences. But it's not as predictable as I would have thought initially; sometimes experienced actors find themselves in the audience, and sometimes very shy people imagine themselves revelling in the spotlight. Some people experience the light as an enemy, and others see it as a friend.

What can we learn about ourselves by asking ourselves this question? Let's walk through and have a look all the choices that appear once we start asking and noticing. First, if we pay attention to our feelings about our thoughts, we might be able to identify some unmet needs. If we feel resentful being in the audience, why is that? Is that a familiar place for us—appreciating other people's work while our own goes unseen? What role would we like to be playing up on that stage?

If we feel deeply anxious about being on stage, what fears are we noticing? What self-talk emerges? Do we feel we don't have the right to be there? Are we scared that we're finally going to be caught out as the pretenders that we've always been? Is there a fear that we're going to disappoint people or make fools of ourselves? Once when working through this image with a client, they said, "I'm feeling guilty because I think I'm about to let down the audience. And I think this is my usual state." The realization hit us both at the same time: that guilt often shows up as a feeling of failing an imaginary audience.

This isn't one of those exercises that slots you into a subtype, like a satisfying online quiz that might tell us what kind of morning routine suits us best. It's more about seeing different parts of ourselves more clearly, and bringing an empathetic awareness to what feels comfortable and what feels uncomfortable. It might also be about finding the sweet spot for ourselves that feels like productive discomfort, which is such an interesting place to be. Let me be clear: avoiding certain kinds of discomfort isn't a bad thing! Some kinds of discomfort or pain will flood us, will bring on toxic stress, or will invoke trauma responses. That's not what we're talking about here.

We're talking about that slightly edgy nervous/excited kind of discomfort, the kind that we might feel at the side of a pool when we're not quite sure of what the temperature is going to be or at the beginning of a conversation that's important and we don't know how it's going to go. It's how we feel when we're facing something uncertain and perhaps important. Learning how to take care of ourselves in these moments of productive discomfort, learning how to stay in and stay present, learning how to resist the urge to avoid or deflect is one of the most exciting and important things we can ever take on. Being able to tolerate that state of productive discomfort can make our worlds so much bigger and more interesting.

If we think about being on stage versus being an audience member, another layer to this thought exercise emerges. What does it feel like when we're experiencing something, and what does it feel like when we're observing? We discussed this earlier when we were exploring the relationships we have with our thoughts and feelings. Cultivating our capacity to shift from the observing self to the experiencing self, to move back and forth seamlessly and gracefully, can transform our daily life and our relationships. We might feel more comfortable in one state than another. For example, we might find ourselves gravitating toward observation. Our ability to notice what we're doing might be very finely honed, so finely honed that it keeps us from enjoying that delicious taste in our mouth, sinking into a connecting moment with someone we love, or hearing a beautiful moment of music and feeling a surge of emotion.

On the other hand, we might be so connected to our experiencing self that we don't notice when we're erasing someone else, or we find ourselves exploding in words or action or diving into something in pursuit of a feeling that ends up causing harm to ourselves or another.

If we accept this invitation to imagine a bright light, and we notice where we are in relation to it, what happens if we play with imagining ourselves in another spot? If our natural impulse is to place ourselves centre stage, what happens if we move into the audience? What helps us make the switch from observed to observer, from centre stage to audience? What does it take for us to start feeling comfortable there, or at the very least, productively uncomfortable? What does it take for those of us who find safety in the audience to move up the aisle and onto the stage? What helps us tolerate this different way of being?

At this point we may be able to identify what the light feels like to us. Does it present as a friend or an enemy? If the light isn't on us, do we feel invisible or unseen? That can be a terrifying feeling—without the light we're invisible and unimportant. We can be curious about what self-talk emerges when the light finds us. If we have a moment of wanting it, of liking it, do we name ourselves as needy or attention-seeking? If the light feels like an enemy, is it because we don't feel safe when attention is placed on us? Perhaps we are used to judgment or criticism, and so that moment of awareness that we are being seen makes us feel particularly vulnerable. Can we appreciate that the light could be attention, and it could also represent connection, understanding, invitation, or appreciation?

I'd like to invite all of us to step into that light for a moment, even those of us who are uncomfortable with it. We may not see ourselves as deserving of (or interested in) a spotlight and may not think we belong on centre stage. Many people struggle with this feeling and end up marginalizing themselves even in the context of their own lives. The fear of being seen as arrogant, as "too much," or as attention-seeking makes them feel like supporting characters in their personal story. If this feels like you, please take a deep breath. Now imagine that bright spotlight on a dark stage, and step right into the centre of it.

Now you're the main character, and it's your feelings, interests, hopes, thoughts, and needs that are most important. You're not stealing space from anyone else; this light has been waiting for you. How familiar are you with your own wants, your own emotions, your own preferences or desires? Are you able to name them clearly, or do you run them first through the filter of other people's needs? Can you gently and without judgment notice if you're doing that and give yourself the experience of directly connecting with your own experience, without feeling the need to accommodate anyone else? If you notice that you talk yourself out of wanting something, can you hit pause and rewind for a few seconds—and then let yourself want what you want?

During this exploration, people often share that they don't really know what they like or want. They're so used to making space for others that they feel completely disconnected from their own preferences. Deep sadness can show up at this point, which we will always make room for, and I get excited for clients when they notice this because it can lead to really joyful experimentation. We can set ourselves little quests to rediscover our favourite tastes, sensations, sounds, smells, experiences, or places, and each time we feel that small dash of delight, we're getting to know ourselves a little better and getting a little more comfortable with the idea that we get to be at the centre of our own story.

Now that we're the main character on our own stage, let's stay up there for a bit and see what else we can notice. Maybe we can take a look at who else is on the stage with us. We might see people who've been cast in different roles, like parent, father, mother, partner, husband, wife, child, daughter, son, boss, or friend. Some of these people seem like a perfect fit for their part, which feels wonderful. In those situations, our interactions feel fluid and natural, and we experience a deep connection and satisfaction.

Others seem miscast; their dialogue might seem off some of the time, or the person may behave in ways that don't align with their role. In some cases, we might notice that our ideas for the part are a mismatch for the person cast in it, and that's okay. We might think about how to change that role to accommodate the person who's playing it, the way directors might give a talented actor room to improvise and play.

For example, we might have an idea about what a best friend is supposed to be based on what we have already experienced or witnessed in our culture or community. The person playing our best friend might not do all those things, but they might do other things very well. Is that a problem with the person or with the role as we understand it? What happens if we adjust our expectations and understanding so that the "best friend" can inhabit the role in a way that makes sense for both them and us?

This way of thinking can be especially helpful for parents who are trying to transform or improve relationships with children. As parents, we often struggle to allow the role of "child" to develop and grow as our child grows, and we weigh it down with layers of expectations and organizing principles that have nothing to do with the individual our child is becoming. If we open the role up to improvisation and experimentation, we may end up with more affirming, authentic, and joyous connections.

In other situations, we might realize a person has been extremely miscast in their part. Someone who should love us is abusive, or someone who should be trustworthy is dishonest. In those situations, when we realize the enormity of the gulf between what we need and what that person can do, we may need to recast that role. That can look like a lot of different things. That can look like ending contact with a person or setting firm boundaries with them. It can look like an internal reorganization of expectations and a restructuring so that that particular role has much less to do. It might also look like recasting someone else in that part, so that the essential job of the role gets done. For example, if the people cast in the roles of parents in our lives aren't able to play their part and love us the way we need them to, we may find other people who can carry out that role for us—partners, friends, or other family members.

We do want to hold this metaphor very lightly, because if we start seeing ourselves as directors or writers with control over a script, we're going to be disappointed. Other people, even people who are perfectly cast in their parts, are not going to recite their lines as expected, and if we can only appreciate or hear the lines we've written we're going to miss out on some beautiful communication. This is more of an improv show than a scripted play.

If we want it to work, we need to let the other actors on the stage know what we need and be willing to make hard choices about who gets to share the stage with us.

"And now on with the show!"

Try this

Take a piece of paper and draw a symbol or shape that represents you right in the middle. Draw symbols that represent people in your life; group and position them according to their relationships to you (and possibly to each other). Now go through and circle the symbols of people you feel really safe and good with. What do you notice? Are the symbols that are closest to you also the ones with the circles? Sometimes they are, and sometimes they aren't. It's just a good thing to notice. If there are symbols with circles that are far away from you on the page, why do you think that is? Is there anything you can do to bring those people closer?

Imagine a string of lights

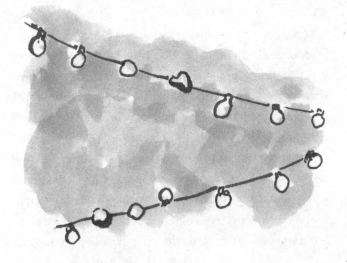

When we look at a string of lights, our attention understandably goes to the brightness. We probably don't see the cord connecting them, and if we do, we might see it as annoying or distracting. Yet the brightness of the lights depends on the presence of the cord.

This image helps me get comfortable with a few ideas, the first being that we cannot live in a state of joy. Joy is something we can move in and out of and treasure when we experience it, but it can't be a permanent state. Attempts to make it permanent will not only not work but will cause us a lot of pain as they fail.

Understanding that joy comes and goes, recognizing that impermanence is an essential part of joy, can help us hold those moments lightly; perhaps it can help us trust that joy will come back, even as we see it going.

Thinking about a string of lights can also help us plan. If we know we're in for a difficult time, we can take a string of lights and stretch it through that tough time of our calendar. What I mean by this is to intentionally schedule things to look forward to, little things and big things, so that you can direct your attention to something that feels delightful or even just a bit better when you need to.

Some of these lights may not shine all that brightly; you may get to the moment and not enjoy it all that much. Joy can't really be prescribed or forced. We are, however, creating opportunities for joy by thinking and planning how to cultivate it.

This is where the thought "hold it lightly" serves us well, especially if we're creating these opportunities for joy for someone else's benefit as well as our own. Just like it's not our fault and not a disaster if one light in the string is a dud, it's okay if something we planned ends up not being all that fun. If we try and force it, if we override our own actual feelings or try to override someone else's feelings, it's not going to work. It's going to build resentment and irritation, which is not what we're after. Shrug, laugh, smile, do whatever else you need to do, express some disappointment if it's there, and do something else. The point wasn't really about the activity itself; it was about opening the door to an opportunity for an emotional experience. If the experience isn't there to be had, that's okay. We close that door and move on.

During the pandemic I really focused on this image of the string of lights. I looked for every relevant awareness day or random holiday to put in the calendar. International Pizza Day? In! Letter Writing Day? Let's try it! We also went on weekly hikes, which everyone in my family grumbled about, then loved, and then grumbled about again as soon as we were done. Having all of these things to look forward to didn't magically make everything easier. Those were incredibly hard days. They did, however, introduce a bit of forward energy into our weeks. They helped replace some of the scaffolding the outer world used to provide for us that had gone missing. Not all of these events were successful; some we gave up on halfway through, some we started preparing for and then stopped, and others ended up being surprisingly lovely.

I think part of what was so important about this practice was that we were pushing against the loss of variability in our days. As much as I rely on gentle scaffolding to get through hard times, I also recognize how important it is to have some differences show up in our day-to-day existence. If everything is the same, day in and day out, we can either start to shut down and deaden our systems and ourselves, or our systems can rebel and demand variability— sometimes in ways that can be destructive. I've seen this with clients who've been frightened by their own behaviours that seem to come out of nowhere, like a usually placid person who erupts in rage in a grocery store. I've also noticed people blowing up their own lives as a response to a feeling of stuckness. They sell their home, leave their partner, quit their job, and they certainly get the variability they were looking for but perhaps a higher dose than they actually wanted.

A middle-path approach may be possible. When we first notice the signs of stuckness, the feeling of day-in, day-out sameness, it might be a cue to invite in some chosen variability, some intentional delight. It might sound contradictory to plan for variability, but really what we're doing is creating space for it. There may be seasons or moments that are always hard; rather than wade through the same challenging experience every time, why not open the door to something new?

Where I live winters can be awful, and I find the months of January to March particularly challenging because they just feel so incredibly long. I do try to get very intentional during these months, stringing my lights through those days and weeks, and it helps. Weekly connections with friends, special meals, movie nights— these things don't magically make me enjoy winter, but sometimes it makes things a little better. Maybe 5 percent, even 10 percent—and that's not nothing.

Try this

I explored this image once with a client, who shared a practice with me that I have in turn told other clients about and have also adopted myself. They put a huge calendar on the wall that has lots of room to write on, and they put everything possible down on the calendar. If they're looking forward to something, they highlight it in their favourite colour.

That colour acts as an instant visual reminder of all the lights they've strung through their weeks. When it's filled in, with just a glance they can get reassurance that there are things to look forward to. They can also see, even from across the room, where there is no colour, and that's an invitation to think about how to add colour or lights to that particular week or month. And finally, at the end of the time frame, whether it's a year or a month or a season, they have a lovely record of all the colour they created and the lights they lit.

Imagine a wave

It's beautiful and sunny, and you're walking along a golden sandy beach. You're feeling light and happy, you see people having fun all around you, and you are thoroughly enjoying this day. Suddenly, an enormous wave rolls in, taking you completely by surprise, and you find yourself tumbling head over heels. The wave rolls out again, leaving you face-first in the sand, perhaps with a bit of stone embedded in your cheek. You stagger to your feet, brush yourself off, and take a deep breath. Maybe you keep walking along that beach, and you might notice that it now feels a little different. Part of you is paying attention to the beach, and part of you is keeping an anxious eye open for the next wave. You might feel scared or angry or resentful that the wave has stolen this experience from you of your perfect golden day.

This wave is any big moment or feeling that can show up suddenly, roll in and roll out again in a matter of seconds, and leave us shaking and shaken as it departs. As it goes, it leaves a shadow or a residue behind, which changes how we see ourselves, the people around us, and the different parts of our lives. I'm in the middle of a grief wave right now as I write this, and I'm noticing my resistance to any thought that feels like it's trivializing this experience. I have no desire to surf this wave or play with it. There's nothing about this that feels playful. It feels elemental and essential.

I find myself wondering about what it might mean to leave the beach, to get away from the wave. I think for the purposes of this metaphor, the beach is where we want to be and how we want to live; it's a place where we experience beauty and connection. Leaving the beach would be moving toward avoidance and isolation. It would mean disconnecting from what's important. For the moment, let's decide that we're staying on the beach because that's where life is.

What happens when we get caught up in a wave? Can we allow ourselves to feel the immensity of it? Can we let it be big? Can we name it as it's happening, that we have been caught up in this huge experience, and can we remember—even as we find ourselves being flipped over and over—that it will not last forever? There's something about knowing it won't last forever that may help us surrender to it while it's happening.

While it's happening, what can we do to tend to ourselves? An image occurs to me of curling up and getting very small, like moving into child's pose or into a fetal position. Maybe I hold onto something that feels solid so that I won't be swept away. I can imagine holding onto someone I love or even bringing my arms around myself. I might squeeze my eyes closed and just let myself be in my own experience for a moment.

Then, as the water rolls out again and the fact that it's leaving registers in my awareness, that might be when I slowly, slowly roll over, take a deep breath, and find a way to get my feet back under me again. Maybe someone's there who can help me get up. Maybe someone else has been through the same thing, and we can hold each other's hands and look into each other's eyes and shout at each other, "What was that!!?? What just happened!? Are you okay? I can't believe what just happened!"

It might be that the person I grab onto doesn't understand what just happened to me. They might tell me to shake it off, get over it or move on—or they might not even grasp that there's been any kind of a wave at all. Part of that might come from their own desire to keep enjoying the beach, to keep seeing it as a safe and beautiful place, or from their discomfort with the idea that I experienced harm. None of that really matters; their perspective is not more important than my experience. I just got knocked over by a wave, and I need a moment.

We can also wonder about where the wave is coming from. Is it originating from outside or inside the self? Some emotions really do appear out of nowhere, just like a freak wave from the sea, caused by events outside of our control. Think of a loved one's death, a lost job, or important plans falling apart. Those moments rush in and take over, and I don't know how possible it is (or even desirable) for a human to withstand them. Instead, those sorts of experiences call for care and time and gentleness and connection.

Sometimes the emotion seems to originate more within the self; something might be happening that sparks a memory or a feeling related to old experiences of harm. These instances can be confusing both to ourselves and to the people around us because our inner experience isn't matching what's going on around us. The wave rises inside, almost secretly, and when it breaks, we don't necessarily get the care that we need (or even understand that we need it).

Thinking about the waves in this way helps me identify what kind of support each experience calls for. Inner waves deserve both care and framing. What I mean by "framing" is an approach that helps us understand why the wave feels as big as it does and helps us process our experience in a way that is workable or livable for us. Inner waves might be well met by different behavioural therapies (like Cognitive Behavioural Therapy or Acceptance Commitment Therapy) or approaches that build brain-body connections (like somatic therapies or EMDR). While we might have many hopes for therapy in these instances, its main job would be to help us know both cognitively and physiologically that while we may be experiencing some cues of danger, we're not in active danger in that moment. Being able to distinguish between what is historic and what is happening in the moment can be one of the greatest gifts of therapy or contemplative practice.

Outer waves need something different, and if we rush to greet them with techniques like cognitive reframing or exposure therapy, we may not get the release that we crave, because the wave can't be reached by our own thoughts or behaviours. If someone else treats our outer wave like an inner wave, we may feel misunderstood or stigmatized. When I worked in the NICU, I sometimes cringed when people would tell the parents of a sick baby that they needed to re-frame their thoughts or face their fears. I wondered if they would be so quick to say that to someone lying by the side of the road after a car accident or to a person standing on the sidewalk watching their house burn down.

I've said already that outer waves need to be met with care, but what does that care look like? We can take some guidance from crisis-support strategies that outline a six-step approach. This works well as a framework to help us ask for the care that we need or to give it to others. The steps are: (1) define the problem (name what happened); (2) address safety needs; (3) provide support; (4) explore alternatives; (5) make plans; and (6) obtain commitment.

Let's think about what this could look like in real life. Imagine that I've just experienced something really hard, like losing my home in some way. Ideally, I would have this dialogue with some-one else, but if no one is available, I can have it with myself. First, I would name what happened and allow myself to understand it as a big thing that deserves space. Then I would think about safety con-cerns. What do I need to be safe? A place to stay? Other resources?

Next, I would require support. Who do I trust? Who can I talk to, and who can help me? What is available for me? Then, I could start evaluating these alternatives. What works best for me right now?

I could start making some real, defined plans as to what happens next, and I would end with making promises to myself about what I'm going to do and when I'm going to do it. If I'm working through this list with someone else, they might be able to help me stay accountable by witnessing my commitment in some way that feels okay for me (i.e., it feels like curiosity and care, not pressure).

Regardless of the origin of the wave, what we need in the moments after the wave has subsided is respectful care. Ideally, we would receive that from those around us, but we can't control that. We can't reach all of those levers. We can, however, make sure to give ourselves respectful care, to notice and honour the emotions we experience, and to give ourselves time to find our feet again.

Try this

There was a lovely tool we used to use in the hospital, which was a self-care plan template. It had spaces to write down names and numbers of people you could call for support, it had ideas for what to do if you found yourself struggling, and it had contact info for relevant services. I think an informal version of this would be great for us all to have. Think of it as an emotional cheat sheet with cues to help us come back into ourselves. It might look something like:

Who do I call?

Where can I go?

What feels like comfort to me?

What movement feels regulating and good for me?

What kind of breath work practice do I like?

If we take a moment to think this through when we're feeling regulated and calm, it might make it easier for us to access these thoughts in times of crisis.

Imagine a spiral

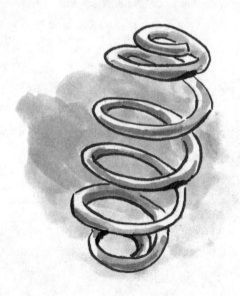

Anniversaries aren't always happy. People often tell me of very complex emotions they experience before the wedding anniversary of a marriage that's now over, before their baby's first birthday when the birth was traumatic, before the one-year mark of an unwanted retirement, or before other painful dates marking change, loss, death, or harm. They feel stuck in the same place with the same shame or grief, and the presence of these similar feelings makes it seem like they'll never be able to move past their pain.

In these moments, it's important to slow down and show ourselves deep compassion. As we moved through the year toward this date and the seasons changed around us, we have been remembering either overtly or subconsciously what was happening at the same time last year. Maybe we got incredibly close to a fire that almost burned us all the way up. If we stop and think about it at all, we can probably feel the heat even now. Of course, we're going to have big feelings about it.

If we want to move through the sense of stuckness, we must first spend some time honouring and naming what we are actually feeling. Anger, sadness, frustration, envy, resentment, grief—they all get a place at the table. Once they've all had a chance to speak, to be seen and heard, then space can open up to notice change. What have we learned? What new parts of ourselves have we discovered? Can we invite them to the table as well? What we are feeling may be familiar, but is it the same? Are we stuck in a circle, condemned to repeat the same feelings and responses over and over again? Or are we in an upward spiral, where we move through these familiar moments but with forward momentum, always ascending?

Do you remember when we were talking about scaffolding, and I shared the story of when I crawled up and down the stairs when my daughter was in the NICU? For years I attached a terrible meaning to that story; it represented a moment of "craziness" that felt deeply scary. I was finally able to learn to hold it differently, and it became a moment I think of tenderly, when my body took over and gave my system something it needed.

My dad died recently, and everything happened so fast that my mind and body could not keep pace with each other. I am profoundly grateful that we were all able to be with him when he died. I know that's a privilege that many long for and few get to experience. That truth is a powerful anchor for me.

It is also true that moving back and forth across the country, in and out of intensely emotional events mixed with practical tasks and everyday existence, left me exhausted and confused. Back home just days after his death, I was standing at the stove ready to make some breakfast when I was suddenly overwhelmed by a tidal wave of grief. I resisted it for a moment, and then all the changed parts of me let me know it was okay to feel this. I sank down on the floor and sobbed. My family came to care for me, and I felt so much grief but also so much connection.

There is something so beautiful about when we see ourselves, when we catch ourselves, in these moments of change. If we reflect for a moment on the metaphor of the box of hand-me-downs or the image of the all-you-can-eat buffet, we can see that there are moments in life when we truly have very few choices or even none at all. That is part of trauma, I think, to be in a moment where no movement is available to you, no moveable pieces, no options other than to endure. Those moments have such impact, and they can teach us important lessons about how to endure, for sure, but endurance does not have to remain our only choice going forward. We don't always have to eat what's forced upon us, and we aren't stuck with a menu with only a few items. In time, with compassion, attention, awareness, and discernment, we can begin to see the extravagant smorgasbord in front of us, the beautiful variety of choices available to us, many of which are there because of our own growth and work.

In fact, the number of choices we have can become overwhelming, so overwhelming that we may want to retreat to the simplicity we're used to, even if it doesn't serve our lives in the present moment. Those are the moments to call into mind the image of the spiral.

What does it look like to give ourselves a pause and then move through this moment, to resist the urge to retreat to the known, and instead take tentative, lovely, slow, uneven, imperfect steps toward something a little bit different, a little more complicated? Let's resist the slide back into the familiar, the inevitable, the singular choice. We may have to scramble a little and the whole thing might look a little messy and inelegant, but an interesting life, one so full of options and possibilities, waits for us if we're willing to try.

As I was writing this book, I imagined it as a kind of conversation, something that might begin a process but not necessarily complete it. These metaphors and explorations have helped me immensely, and I've seen how they've helped others get unhooked from unworkable patterns. What is always wonderful is to see where people go from there and where their own imaginations take them.

My hope is that you hear the invitation in this book, feel the friendly encouragement, and see the outstretched hand that's there and ready when you are. These words and these images can help you meet up with some wonderful parts of yourself that you haven't seen in a long time, recognize your own capacities—some of which you haven't yet had a chance to explore fully—and give yourself the beautiful care that you've always deserved but perhaps have never received. What will happen when you change your relationship with the thoughts that hold you down and find a way to move forward that looks and feels like you? What could happen next? I am so excited for you to find out.

Acknowledgements

I want to thank the incomparable Nicole Winstanley for her editorial guidance and her deep kindness. What a pleasure it has been to get to work with you! I must also extend gratitude to the many wonderful team members at Simon & Schuster. To Kaitlyn Lonnee and Chloe Gandy—I appreciate all that you have done for this book and for me. To Sebastian Frye—I'm so grateful for your thoughtful design work and your exquisite illustrations. You've made this book so beautiful. To Carolyn Forde at Transatlantic—thank you for your wisdom and support. I feel so lucky to have you in my corner.

I'm very fortunate to be part of a few different communities who've held me up during hard times, like my beloved NICU family at Sunnybrook. To Elizabeth MacMillan-York—thank you for catching us all before we fell. To the Canadian Premature Babies Foundation and the Canadian Preemie Parent Support Network—I'm so proud of us all for creating such a generous, warmhearted supportive space. Fabiana Bacchini—I am in awe of all that you've done. To my therapy friends from the Toronto Institute of Relational Psychotherapy—I don't miss group process, but I do miss you. To Jennifer Kalb, who has guided me as I began my private practice, and to Paula Klein, who has been such a lighthouse figure for me over the last few years—my deepest thanks. To all my clients—it's such a privilege to get to spend time with you.

There are so many people who've inspired me with their work—some of whom I've been fortunate enough to meet and get to know and some whom I've appreciated from afar—Vania Sukola, Jessie Herrold, Jo-Ann Alfred, Pema Chodron, Sebene Selassie, Lesley Barreira, Julia Orkin, Linda Thai, Russ Harris, Stan Tatkin, Mariame Kaba, Steven Hayes, KC Davis, Adrienne Maree Brown, Ann Douglas, Nedra Glover Tawwab, Anne Lamott, Oliver Burkeman, Hope Edelman, Richard Schwartz, James Hollis—this could be a much longer list, but I need to say thanks for your generosity in sharing your wisdom with the world in the way that you do.

I'm so grateful for my beautiful friends, who kept me company along the way—Jack Hourigan, Nancy Cardwell, Katrina Onstad, Jody Chan, Stephanie Hodnett, Alison McLennan, Steve Pratt, Adrian McKerracher, Elisa Vicencio, Jessica Reid, Ted Burns, Seanna Rishor and Kate Hilton. To Sarah Polley—none of this would have happened without you. Your kindness and curiosity helped me get brave.

I'm so lucky to have a wonderful family spread across the country, from British Columbia to Nova Scotia, and I love and thank you all. To my dear sister Jennifer, you have been so supportive and also so inspiring. You helped me believe this could happen.

To Sean—thank you for your loving heart and steady presence. To Maggie-Lis and Grace—I am endlessly proud of you and so completely delighted by you. When I think of you three, I remember who I want to be.

About the Author

GRACE JENSEN

KATE ROBSON is a Registered Psychotherapist in Toronto, Ontario. Inspired by her own experiences with her children in a Neonatal Intensive Care Unit, she worked with babies, parents, and families for more than twelve years as an NICU Family Support Specialist. She's travelled all over the world educating parents and clinicians about family-centred care and trauma-informed care practices. Her workshops focus on cultivating attachment in relationships and creating emotion-friendly homes and workplaces. In her private practice she supports individuals and couples experiencing infertility, high-risk pregnancies, NICU hospitalizations, and bereavement. She co-manages Canada's largest support community for NICU families and runs a weekly support group for parents and caregivers. She has degrees from McGill University and OISE at the University of Toronto, completed her psychotherapy training at the Toronto Institute for Relational Psychotherapy, and has also studied modalities such as Acceptance Commitment Therapy (ACT), the Internal Family Systems model, Eye Movement Desensitization and Reprocessing (EMDR), Psychobiological Approach to Couple Therapy (PACT), and somatic embodiment.